Better Homes and Gardens®

QUILT-LOVERS' FAVORITES®

FROM AMERICAN PATCHWORK & QUILTING™

Better Homes and Gardens® Creative Collection®
Des Moines, Iowa

VOLUME 10

Editor in Chief	DEBORAH GORE OHRN
Executive Editor	JENNIFER ERBE KELTNER
Art Director	TIM ALEXANDER
Creative Director	BRENDA DRAKE LESCH

Better Homes and Gardens

QUILT-LOVERS' FAVORITES

FROM AMERICAN PATCHWORK & QUILTING

Senior Editor ELIZABETH TISINGER		*Design Director* NANCY WILES	
Editor JILL ABELOE MEAD		*Senior Graphic Designer* ELIZABETH STUMBO	
Assistant Editor JODY SANDERS		*Contributing Graphic Designer* JANN WILLIAMS	
Interactive Editor LISA SCHUMACHER		*Contributing Technical Illustrator* CHRIS NEUBAUER GRAPHICS	
Staff Writer MARIA V. SCHWAMMAN		*Contributing Watercolor Illustrator* ANN WEISS	
Contributing Quilt Tester LAURA BOEHNKE		*Contributing Photo Stylist* TARI COLBY	
Contributing Technical Editor LILA TAYLOR SCOTT		*Administrative Assistant* MARY IRISH	
Contributing Project Designer		JAN RAGALLER	
Contributing Copy Editors		MARY HEATON AND MARY HELEN SCHILTZ	
Contributing Proofreader		ELLEN MODERSOHN	
Contributing Writers		DIANE DORO, ANGELA INGLE, AND HEIDI KAISAND	

Group Director, Premedia/Quality Operations	STEVE JOHNSON
Senior Director, Premedia Services	PENNY SULLIVAN
Color Quality Analyst	PAM POWERS
Prepress Desktop Specialist	GREG FAIRHOLM
Consumer Products Marketing Director	STEVE SWANSON
Consumer Products Marketing Manager	WENDY MERICAL
Business Director	RON CLINGMAN
Assoc. Director Book Manufacturing	DOUGLAS M. JOHNSTON

Vice President and General Manager, SIP	JEFF MYERS
Brand Manager	MARK MOOBERRY
Marketing Director, Meredith Direct	HEATHER PROCTOR

Meredith National Media Group

President	JACK GRIFFIN
EXECUTIVE VICE PRESIDENTS	
President of Consumer Magazines	TOM HARTY
Chief Brand Officer	ANDY SAREYAN
Chief Digital Officer	DOUG OLSON
President, Meredith Integrated Marketing	MARTIN F. REIDY
SENIOR VICE PRESIDENTS	
Chief Marketing Officer	NANCY WEBER
Consumer Marketing	DAVID BALL
Corporate Sales	MICHAEL BROWNSTEIN
Editorial Director, Des Moines	GAYLE GOODSON BUTLER
Editorial Director, New York	SALLY LEE
Finance	MIKE RIGGS
Meredith 360°	JEANNINE SHAO COLLINS
Meredith Women's Network	LAUREN WIENER
VICE PRESIDENTS	
Chief Technology Officer	TINA STEIL
Direct Response and Travel	PATTI FOLLO
New Media and Marketing Services	ANDY WILSON
Newsstand	DAVID ALGIRE
Production	BRUCE HESTON
Research Solutions	BRITTA WARE

✷ meredith

President, Chief Executive Officer STEPHEN M. LACY

Chairman of the Board WILLIAM T. KERR

In Memoriam — E.T. MEREDITH III (1933–2003)

SOMETHING FOR EVERYONE

Intricate or simple. Appliquéd or pieced. Antique or modern. Whether you plan to make an heirloom to pass on to future generations or need an on-the-fly gift for a friend, you'll find exactly what you're looking for in our latest edition, Volume 10, of Quilt-Lovers' Favorites®.

In this book you'll find 15 of our most popular patterns from past issues of American Patchwork & Quilting® *magazine and its sister publications. To prove the possibilities are endless, we present more than 30 all-new projects using the blocks, units, borders, or appliqué shapes from the original quilts. There are tiny treasures, bed-size beauties, and everything in between. We also offer color options to show how you can customize a pattern to your tastes with different fabrics and combinations.*

To make the process easier, we include clear and concise instructions, full-size patterns, and a reference guide to quiltmaking—Quilter's Schoolhouse, page 156. *Our charts of optional sizes further help you customize each project.*

Our goal is to give you the confidence you need to make exactly what you want. My guess is that the most challenging part of the process will be deciding which project to make first!

Jennifer Erbe Keltner
Executive Editor, American Patchwork & Quilting

3

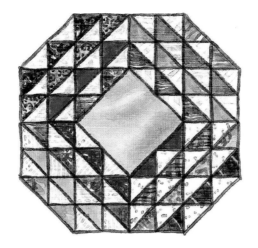

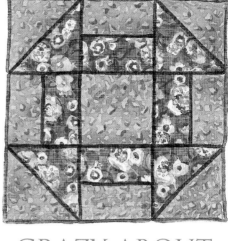

TABLE *of* CONTENTS

FUTURE HEIRLOOMS
Page **6**

CRAZY ABOUT COLOR
Page **40**

4

28

14

36

30

FUTURE HEIRLOOMS

New techniques evolve and trends come and go, but some designs will never go out of style. These ageless patterns allow you to honor quilts of the past while putting your own spin on history. Re-create the look of the timeless classics on the following pages to leave a lasting treasure for generations to come.

LINKS TO *Home*

Remember the quilts you snuggled under at Grandmother's house? Chances are the Irish Chain pattern was among them. Create your own lasting heirloom when you make your version of this Triple Irish Chain throw from quilt collector Miriam Kujac.

Materials

5 yards muslin (blocks, inner and outer borders, binding)

2¼ yards solid red (blocks, middle border)

1⅛ yards solid Cheddar yellow (blocks)

4¾ yards backing fabric

77×85" batting

Finished quilt: 70¼×79"
Finished block: 8¾" square

Quantities are for 44/45"-wide, 100% cotton fabrics. **Measurements** include ¼" seam allowances. Sew with right sides together unless otherwise stated.

Collector Notes

The combination of red and Cheddar yellow drew collector and quilter Miriam Kujac to this quilt. Always on the lookout for wonderful quilts to add to her collection, she found this one at the Farmington Antiques Weekend in Farmington, Connecticut.

"Even though there's a small number of stitches per inch, the hand quilting is lovely and shows up well," she says, "especially the floral wreaths in the muslin squares."

Cut Fabrics

Cut pieces in the following order.

To make the best use of each fabric, we've specified both 42"-long and 21"-long strip sets.

From muslin, cut:
- 4—4¼×42" strips
- 8—2½×42" binding strips
- 42—1¾×42" strips
- 2—4¼×21" strips
- 16—1¾×21" strips
- 28—6¾" squares

From solid red, cut:
- 8—2¼×42" strips for middle border
- 20—1¾×42" strips
- 11—1¾×21" strips

From solid Cheddar yellow, cut:
- 13—1¾×42" strips
- 7—1¾×21" strips

continued

Assemble Strip Sets

1. Referring to **Diagram 1**, sew together three muslin 1¾×42" strips, two solid red 1¾×42" strips, and two solid Cheddar yellow 1¾×42" strips to make strip set A. Press seams toward red and yellow strips. Repeat to make a second strip set A. Using 1¾×21" strips, make a third strip set A.

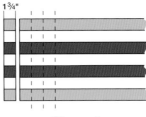

1¾"

Diagram 1
Strip Set A

2. Cut A strip sets into a total of 56—1¾"-wide A segments.

3. Sew together four muslin 1¾×42" strips, a solid red 1¾×42" strip, and two solid Cheddar yellow 1¾×42" strips to make strip set B **(Diagram 2)**. Press seams toward red and yellow strips. Repeat to make a second strip set B. Using 1¾×21" strips, make a third strip set B.

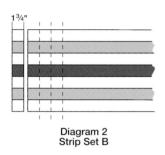

Diagram 2
Strip Set B

4. Cut B strip sets into a total of 56—1¾"-wide B segments.

5. Sew together three muslin 1¾×42" strips, two solid red 1¾×42" strips, and two solid Cheddar yellow 1¾×42" strips to make strip set C **(Diagram 3)**. Press seams toward red and yellow strips. Repeat to make a second strip set C. Using 1¾×21" strips, make a third strip set C.

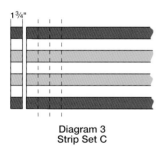

Diagram 3
Strip Set C

6. Cut C strip sets into a total of 56—1¾"-wide C segments.

7. Join four muslin 1¾×42" strips, two solid red 1¾×42" strips, and a solid Cheddar yellow 1¾×42"

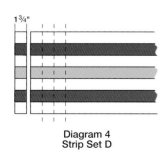

Diagram 4
Strip Set D

strip to make strip set D **(Diagram 4)**. Press seams toward red and yellow strips. Using 1¾×21" strips, make a second strip set D.

8. Cut D strip sets into a total of 28—1¾"-wide D segments.

9. Sew solid red 1¾×42" strips to long edges of a muslin 4¼×42" strip to make strip set E **(Diagram 5)**. Press seams toward red strips. Repeat to make a second strip set E. Using 21"-long strips, make a third strip set E.

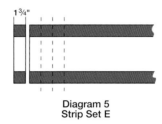

Diagram 5
Strip Set E

10. Cut E strip sets into a total of 56—1¾"-wide E segments.

11. Sew together two muslin 1¾×42" strips, two solid red 1¾×42" strips, and a muslin 4¼×42" strip to make strip set F **(Diagram 6)**. Press seams toward red strips. Repeat to make a second strip set F. Using 21"-long strips, make a third strip set F.

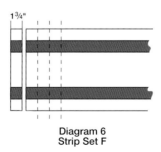

Diagram 6
Strip Set F

12. Cut F strip sets into a total of 56—1¾"-wide F segments.

Assemble Blocks

1. Referring to **Diagram 7**, sew together two A segments, two B segments, two C segments,

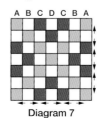

A B C D C B A

Diagram 7

continued

and one D segment to make a checkerboard block. Press seams as indicated by arrows on diagram. The block should be 9¼" square including seam allowances. Repeat to make 28 checkerboard blocks total.

2. Sew E segments to opposite edges of a muslin 6¾" square (**Diagram 8**). Press seams toward E segments. Add F segments to remaining edges to make a setting block. Press seams toward muslin square. The setting block should be 9¼" square including seam allowances. Repeat to make 28 setting blocks total.

Diagram 8

Assemble Quilt Center
1. Referring to **Quilt Assembly Diagram**, lay out checkerboard blocks and setting blocks in eight rows, alternating blocks.

2. Sew together blocks in each row. Press seams toward setting blocks.

3. Join rows to make quilt center. Press seams in one direction. The quilt center should be 61¼×70½" including seam allowances.

Add Borders
1. Cut and piece muslin 1¾×42" strips to make:
- 2—1¾×79" outer border strips
- 2—1¾×73" inner border strips
- 2—1¾×67¾" outer border strips
- 2—1¾×61¼" inner border strips

2. Sew short inner border strips to short edges of quilt center. Add long inner border strips to remaining edges. Press all seams toward inner border.

3. Cut and piece solid red 2¼×42" strips to make:
- 2—2¼×76½" middle border strips
- 2—2¼×64¼" middle border strips

Quilt Assembly Diagram

Quilting Diagram

Links to Home

4. Sew short middle border strips to short edges of quilt center. Add long middle border strips to remaining edges. Press all seams toward middle border.

5. Sew short outer border strips to short edges of quilt center. Add long outer border strips to remaining edges to complete quilt top. Press all seams toward middle border.

Finish Quilt

1. Layer quilt top, batting, and backing; baste. (For details, see Complete Quilt, *page 159*.)

2. Quilt as desired. This antique quilt is hand-quilted with a diagonal grid running through the center of each square in the checkerboard blocks. The grid lines running from upper left to lower right continue into the border, forming parallel diagonal lines **(Quilting Diagram)**. A floral wreath design is hand-quilted in the setting squares.

3. Bind with muslin binding strips. (For details, see Complete Quilt.)

LINKS TO HOME
optional sizes

If you'd like to make this quilt in a size other than a throw, use the information *below*.

Alternate quilt sizes	Wall/Lap	Full/Queen	King
Number of checkerboard blocks	12	45	60
Number of setting blocks	13	45	61
Number of blocks wide by long	5×5	9×10	11×11
Finished size	52¾" square	87¾×96½"	105¼" square

Yardage Requirements			
Muslin	3 yards	6⅝ yards	9⅛ yards
Solid red	1¼ yards	2⅜ yards	3½ yards
Solid Cheddar yellow	½ yard	1½ yards	1⅞ yards
Backing	3⅓ yards	7⅞ yards	9⅓ yards
Batting	59" square	94×103"	112" square

optional colors

Flower Power

Florals, a pseudo-stripe, and paisley prints take a playful turn around quilt tester Laura Boehnke's wall hanging version of *Links to Home*.

"As soon as I saw the elaborate pink stripe fabric, I knew I wanted to use it for a mitered border," Laura says. "It reminds me of an ornate frame." (See Miter Borders on *page 158* for instructions on how to achieve this look.) "I also used a large floral print in place of the muslin," she says. "It lessens the contrast and minimizes the graphic X that pops out on the original quilt, softening the design a bit overall."

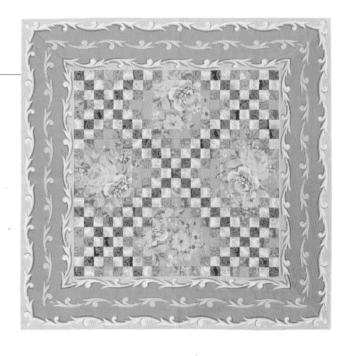

QUILT OF MANY COLORS

Mulitcolor-stripe fabric gives a classic pattern a modern edge

on this geometric quilt that will brighten up any space.

Materials

2¾ yards dark multicolor stripe (blocks, border,

    binding)

2 yards total assorted multicolor stripes (blocks)

2½ yards total assorted bright solids (blocks)

4½ yards backing fabric

79" square batting

Finished quilt: 72¾" square

Cut Fabrics

Cut pieces in the order that follows in each section. Cut border strips lengthwise (parallel to the selvages).

From dark multicolor stripe, cut:
- 4—6×75" border strips
- 8—2½×42" binding strips

From assorted multicolor stripes and scraps of dark multicolor stripe, cut:
- 49—6¾" squares

Assemble Blocks

The instructions that follow result in one block. Repeat cutting and assembly steps to make 49 blocks total.

From one assorted bright solid, cut:
- 8—1¾" squares

From a second assorted bright solid, cut:
- 4—1¾×4¼" rectangles
- 4—1¾" squares

1. Referring to **Diagram 9**, sew together two solid No. 1—1¾" squares and one solid No. 2—1¾×4¼" rectangle to make a short segment. Press seams open. Repeat to make a second short segment.

Diagram 9

2. Referring to **Diagram 10**, sew together two solid No. 1—1¾" squares, two solid No. 2—1¾" squares, and one solid No. 2—1¾×4¼" rectangle to make a long segment. Press seams open. Repeat to make a second long segment.

Diagram 10

3. Sew short segments to opposite edges of an assorted multicolor stripe or dark multicolor stripe 6¾" square (**Diagram 11**). Add long segments to remaining edges to make a block. Press all seams open. The block should be 9¾" square including seam allowances.

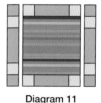

Diagram 11

Assemble Quilt Top

1. Referring to photo on *page 16,* lay out blocks in seven rows, rotating direction of stripes in block centers.

2. Sew together blocks in each row. Press seams in one direction, alternating direction with each row. Join rows to make quilt center. Press seams in one direction. The quilt center should be 61¾" square including seam allowances.

3. Sew border strips to opposite edges of quilt center, starting and stopping ¼" from corners of quilt center. Add remaining border strips, mitering corners, to complete quilt top. (For details, see Miter Borders, *page 158.*) Press all seams toward border.

Finish Quilt

1. Layer quilt top, batting, and backing; baste. (For details, see Complete Quilt, *page 159.*)

2. Quilt as desired. Continuous spiral designs are stitched across the featured quilt.

3. Bind with dark multicolor stripe binding strips. (For details, see Complete Quilt.)

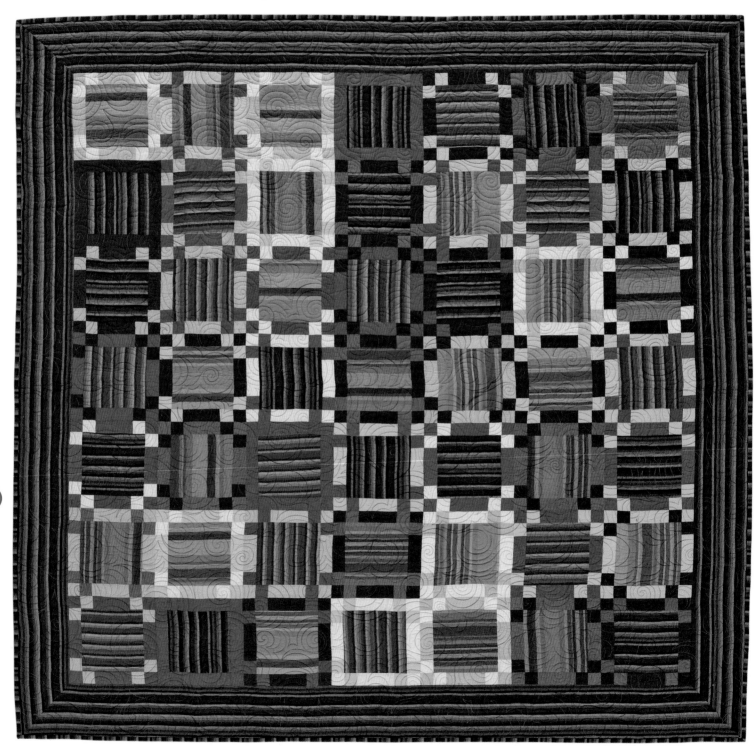

SAFARI-PRINT THROW

Fussy-cut a jungle-theme print to showcase hidden critters in the setting blocks.

Materials

1⅛ yards solid black (blocks, binding)

1¾ yards rust print (blocks)

1⅛ yards green print (blocks)

⅞ yard novelty print (blocks)

2⅞ yards backing fabric

51" square batting

Finished quilt: 44¼" square

Cut Fabrics

Cut pieces in the following order.

From solid black, cut:
- 5—2½×42" binding strips
- 7—1¾×42" strips
- 6—1¾×12" strips

From rust print, cut:
- 2—4¼×42" strips
- 2—4¼×12" strips
- 16—1¾×42" strips
- 12—1¾×12" strips

From green print, cut:
- 11—1¾×42" strips
- 9—1¾×12" strips

From novelty print, cut:
- 13—6¾" squares

Assemble Strip Sets

Refer to **Diagrams 12** and **13** for color placement in each strip set.

1. Referring to Assemble Strip Sets, Step 1, *page 10,* use two solid black 1¾×42" strips, three rust print 1¾×42" strips, and two green print 1¾×42" strips to make strip set A. Using 1¾×12" strips, make a second strip set A. Cut A strip sets into a total of 24—1¾"-wide A segments.

2. Referring to Assemble Strip Sets, Step 3, *page 11,* use four rust print 1¾×42" strips, two solid black 1¾×42" strips, and one green print 1¾×42" strip to make strip set B. Using 1¾×12" strips, make a second strip set B. Cut B strip sets into a total of 24—1¾"-wide B segments.

3. Referring to Assemble Strip Sets, Step 5, use two green print 1¾×42" strips, three rust print 1¾×42" strips, and two solid black 1¾×42" strips to make strip set C. Using 1¾×12" strips, make a second strip set C. Cut C strip sets into a total of 24—1¾"-wide C segments.

4. Referring to Assemble Strip Sets, Step 7, use four rust print 1¾×42" strips, two green print 1¾×42" strips, and one solid black 1¾×42" strip to make strip set D. Cut D strip set into a total of 12—1¾"-wide D segments.

5. Referring to Assemble Strip Sets, Step 9, use two green print 1¾×42" strips and a rust print 4¼×42" strip to make strip set E. Using 4¼×12" strips, make a second strip set E. Cut E strip sets into 26—1¾"-wide E segments total.

6. Referring to Assemble Strip Sets, Step 11, use two rust print 1¾×42" strips, two green print 1¾×42" strips, and a rust print 4¼×42" strip to make strip set F. Using 4¼×12" strips, make a second strip set F. Cut F strip sets into 26—1¾"-wide F segments total.

Assemble Blocks

1. Referring to Assemble Blocks, Step 1, *page 11,* use A–D segments to make a checkerboard block **(Diagram 12)**. Repeat to make 12 checkerboard blocks total.

2. Referring to Assemble Blocks, Step 2, *page 12,* use a novelty print 6¾" square and E and F segments to make a setting block **(Diagram 13)**. Repeat to make 13 setting blocks total.

Assemble Quilt Top

1. Referring to photo *opposite,* lay out checkerboard blocks and setting blocks in five rows, alternating blocks.

2. Sew together pieces in each row. Press seams toward setting blocks. Join rows to complete quilt top. Press seams in one direction.

Finish Quilt

1. Layer quilt top, batting, and backing; baste. (For details, see Complete Quilt, *page 159*.)

2. Quilt as desired. This quilt is stitched with an allover spiral design.

3. Bind with solid black binding strips. (For details, see Complete Quilt.)

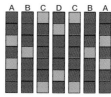

Diagram 12

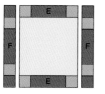

Diagram 13

KENTUCKY
Sunburst

Poison-green sashing sets off the sparkling pieced sunbursts in this mid-19th-century quilt found in Kentucky. The pink-and-neutral print sunrays contrast nicely with dark print backgrounds and the unifying red plaid used throughout.

Materials

⅝ yard total assorted pink prints (blocks)

⅝ yard total assorted white, light gray, and light tan prints (blocks)

2⅛ yards total assorted brown and black prints (blocks)

3⅝ yards red plaid (blocks, sashing)

3½ yards green print (sashing, border, binding)

5⅓ yards backing fabric

78×95" batting

Finished quilt: 72×89"
Finished block: 12½" square

Quantities are for 44/45"-wide, 100% cotton fabrics. **Measurements** include ¼" seam allowances. Sew with right sides together unless otherwise stated.

Designer Notes

Although the unknown designer of this quilt apparently had a plan to make each sunburst block with a red plaid center, pink sunrays alternating with light print sunrays, and a background of black or brown, she didn't hesitate to combine fabrics when she didn't have enough of one. She combined fabrics that look similar, so when blocks are viewed from a distance, the mixtures are unnoticeable.

Cut Fabrics

Cut pieces in the following order. Patterns are on *Pattern Sheet 2*. To make templates of patterns, see Make and Use Templates, *page 156*. Be sure to transfer dots marked on patterns A and B to templates, then to fabric pieces. Dots are matching points and are used to join pieces. Be sure to add a ³⁄₁₆" seam allowance when cutting out appliqué piece C.

From assorted pink prints, cut:
- 140 of Pattern A (20 sets of 7)

From assorted white, light gray, and light tan prints, cut:
- 140 of Pattern A (20 sets of 7)

From assorted brown and black prints, cut:
- 280 of Pattern B (20 sets of 14)

From red plaid, cut:
- 80 of Pattern D
- 20 of Pattern C
- 12—5" sashing squares

From green print, cut:
- 9—4½×42" strips for border
- 9—2½×42" binding strips
- 31—5×13" sashing rectangles

continued

Assemble Blocks

1. For one block you'll need seven A points from one pink print, seven A points from one light print, 14 B wedges from one black or brown print, a red plaid C circle, and four red plaid D pieces.

2. Carefully aligning matching points, pin a pink print A point to a black or brown print B wedge. Sew together to make a pink sunray unit, being careful not to stretch the bias edges **(Diagram 1)**. Press seam toward B piece. Repeat to make seven pink sunray units total.

Diagram 1

3. Repeat Step 2 with light print A points and remaining black or brown print B wedges to make seven light sunray units total.

4. Lay out the 14 sunray units in a circle, alternating pink and light units. Carefully aligning matching points, join sunray units to make a donut unit **(Diagram 2)**. Press seams toward A points.

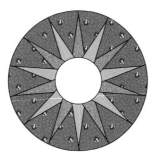

Diagram 2

5. Press under $\frac{3}{16}$" seam allowance on red plaid C circle. Position prepared circle over opening in donut unit **(Diagram 3)**. Using matching thread, slip-stitch circle in place to make a sunburst unit.

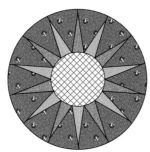

Diagram 3

6. Sew together four red plaid D pieces to make a square frame **(Diagram 4)**. Press seams open.

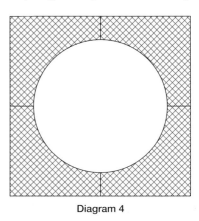

Diagram 4

7. Press under $\frac{1}{4}$" seam allowance on sunburst unit. Position prepared unit over opening in square frame, aligning frame's vertical seams with two sunburst points **(Diagram 5)**. Slip-stitch sunburst unit to frame to make a sunburst block. The block should be 13" square including seam allowances.

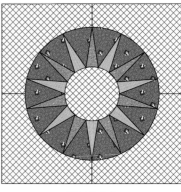

Diagram 5

8. Repeat steps 1–7 to make 20 sunburst blocks total.

Assemble Quilt Center

1. Referring to photo *opposite,* lay out sunburst blocks, green print sashing rectangles, and red plaid sashing squares in nine horizontal rows. (In the featured quilt, about half the blocks are rotated 90 degrees; star points will either align with the blocks's vertical or horizontal seam.) Sew together pieces in each row. Press seams toward sashing rectangles.

Kentucky Sunburst

continued

2. Join rows to make quilt center. Press seams toward sashing rows. The quilt center should be 64×81" including seam allowances.

Add Border

1. Cut and piece green print 4½×42" strips to make:
- 2—4½×89" border strips
- 2—4½×64" border strips

2. Sew short border strips to short edges of quilt center. Sew long border strips to remaining edges to complete quilt top. Press all seams toward border.

Finish Quilt

1. Layer quilt top, batting, and backing; baste. (For details, see Complete Quilt, *page 159*.)

2. Quilt as desired. This antique quilt is quilted with an allover Baptist fan pattern with arcs spaced ¾" apart.

3. Bind with green print binding strips. (For details, see Complete Quilt.)

KENTUCKY SUNBURST
optional sizes

If you'd like to make this quilt in a size other than for a twin-size bed, use the information *below*.

Alternate quilt sizes	Wall/Lap	Full/Queen	King
Number of blocks	9	30	36
Number of blocks wide by long	3×3	5×6	6×6
Finished size	55" square	89×106"	106" square

Yardage Requirements

Total assorted pink prints	⅜ yard	¾ yard	⅞ yard
Total assorted white, light gray, and light tan prints	⅜ yard	¾ yard	⅞ yard
Total assorted brown and black prints	1¼ yards	3⅛ yards	3¾ yards
Red plaid	1¼ yards	5 yards	5⅞ yards
Green print	2⅛ yards	4¾ yards	5⅓ yards
Backing	3½ yards	8 yards	9⅓ yards
Batting	61" square	95×112"	112" square

optional colors

Sizzling Summertime Fun

Quilt tester Laura Boehnke had hot summer days on her mind when she re-created this project using sunny yellows, hot pink, and ocean blue fabrics. The bright, intense colors on a dark background dramatically change the quilt's look.

BIG-BLOCK PICNIC THROW

Replace sunbursts with large square blocks to showcase a flirty, feminine floral.

Materials

2⅓ yards green floral (large squares)

18x22" piece (fat quarter) purple print (sashing)

2⅓ yards yellow tone-on-tone (sashing, inner
   border)

2⅓ yards multicolor stripe (outer border, binding)

7½ yards backing fabric

89" square batting

Finished quilt: 83" square

Cut Fabrics

Cut pieces in the following order.

From green floral, cut:
- 16—13" squares

From purple print, cut:
- 9—5" sashing squares

From yellow tone-on-tone, cut:
- 8—4½×42" strips for inner border
- 24—5×13" sashing rectangles

From multicolor stripe, cut:
- 9—6×42" strips for outer border
- 9—2½×42" binding strips

Assemble Quilt Top

1. Referring to photo, *opposite,* lay out green floral
13" squares, purple print sashing squares, and
yellow tone-on-tone sashing rectangles in seven
rows.

2. Sew together pieces in each row. Press seams
toward sashing rectangles. Join rows to make
quilt center. Press seams in one direction. The
quilt center should be 64" square including seam
allowances.

3. Cut and piece yellow tone-on-tone 4½×42" strips
to make:
- 2—4½×72" inner border strips
- 2—4½×64" inner border strips

4. Sew short inner border strips to opposite edges
of quilt center. Add long inner border strips to
remaining edges. Press all seams toward inner
border.

5. Cut and piece multicolor stripe 6×42" strips
to make:
- 2—6×83" outer border strips
- 2—6×72" outer border strips

6. Sew short outer border strips to opposite edges
of quilt center. Add long outer border strips to
remaining edges to complete quilt top. Press all
seams toward outer border.

Finish Quilt

1. Layer quilt top, batting, and backing; baste.
(For details, see Complete Quilt, *page 159.*)

2. Quilt as desired. The featured quilt is machine-
quilted with a wave and feather designs in the
green floral squares and a flower motif in each
sashing square. Feather designs highlight the
sashing rectangles and outer border, and a spiral
pattern appears in the outer border.

3. Bind with multicolor stripe binding strips.
(For details, see Complete Quilt.)

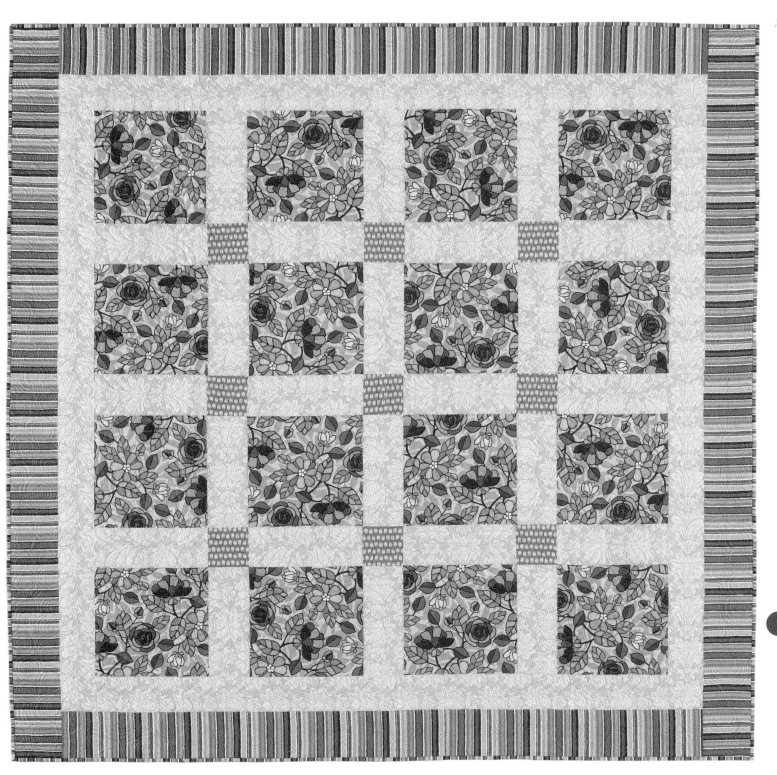

NEUTRAL SILK PILLOW

Splurge on fabric and spotlight one star on a luxurious pillow.

Materials

¾ yard solid gray douppioni silk (block, piping, pillow back)

⅛ yard solid tan douppioni silk (block)

⅛ yard solid cream douppioni silk (block)

13" square white flannel (lining)

1½ yards ½"-diameter cording

Large safety pin

12"-square pillow form

Finished pillow: 13½" square

Cut Fabrics

Cut pieces in the following order. This project uses *Kentucky Sunburst* patterns on *Pattern Sheet 2*.

From solid gray silk, cut:
- 2—13×17" rectangles
- 3—2½×42" strips for piping
- 4 of Pattern D
- 7 of Pattern A

From solid tan silk, cut:
- 7 of Pattern A
- 1 of Pattern C

From solid cream silk, cut:
- 14 of Pattern B

Assemble Pillow Top

1. Referring to Assemble Blocks, steps 2–7, *page 22*, use solid gray silk A and D pieces, solid tan silk A and C pieces, and solid cream silk B pieces to make a sunburst block.

2. Layer white flannel 13" lining square and sunburst block with wrong sides together. Baste together along all edges to make pillow top.

Finish Pillow

1. Cut and piece solid gray silk 2½×42" strips to make a 115"-long strip. Fold under 1" at one short end of strip; press. With wrong side inside, fold strip in half lengthwise. Using a ¼" seam allowance, sew together long edges to make a piping cover.

2. Attach a large safety pin to one end of ½"-diameter cording. Insert pin into folded end of piping cover. Push cording into piping cover, moving safety pin a short distance at a time and forming gathers in piping cover (**Diagram 6**). Arrange gathers evenly along length of cord to make piping.

Diagram 6

3. Aligning raw edges and using a machine zipper foot, stitch piping to right side of pillow top. (For details, see Piping, steps 2 and 3, on *page 159*.)

4. With wrong side inside, fold each solid gray silk 13×17" rectangle in half to make two 8½×13" double-thick pillow back rectangles. Overlap folded edges by about 4" to make a 13"-square pillow back (**Diagram 7**). Baste along top and bottom edges to secure pieces.

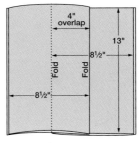

Diagram 7

5. With right sides together, layer pillow top and pillow back; pin or baste edges. Sew together through all layers to make pillow cover, rounding corners slightly.

6. Turn pillow cover right side out through opening in pillow back. Insert 12"-square pillow form.

TIP: *When pressing silk fabric, use a pressing sheet to keep it from discoloring.*

MAKING
Waves

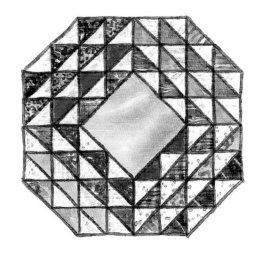

A striking, vintage Ocean Waves quilt from collector Julie Hendricksen combines sky-blue setting pieces, scrappy triangles, and an unexpected touch of pink along the top and bottom.

Materials

1¾ yards solid blue (setting squares, setting triangles, corner triangles)

⅔ yard solid white (binding)

⅞ yard total assorted pink prints (Ocean Waves units)

3⅞ yards total assorted medium to dark prints in blue, green, red, yellow, and black (Ocean Waves units)

3⅓ yards total assorted light prints (Ocean Waves units)

4¾ yards backing fabric

73×85" batting

Finished quilt: 66½×78½"

Quantities are for 44/45" wide, 100% cotton fabrics. **Measurements** include ¼" seam allowances. Sew with right sides together unless otherwise stated.

Cut Fabrics

Cut pieces in the order that follows in each section.

From solid blue, cut:
- 6—7¼" squares, cutting each diagonally twice in an X for 24 setting triangles total (you will use 22)
- 60—4¾" setting squares
- 1—3⅞" square, cutting it in half diagonally for 2 corner triangles total

From solid white, cut:
- 8—2½×42" binding strips

Cut and Assemble Ocean Waves Units

For each Ocean Waves unit, the unknown maker of this antique quilt used four medium or dark prints and one pink or light print.

Pink Ocean Waves Units

The following instructions result in two identical pink Ocean Waves units. Repeat cutting and assembly instructions to make 24 pink Ocean Waves units total.

continued

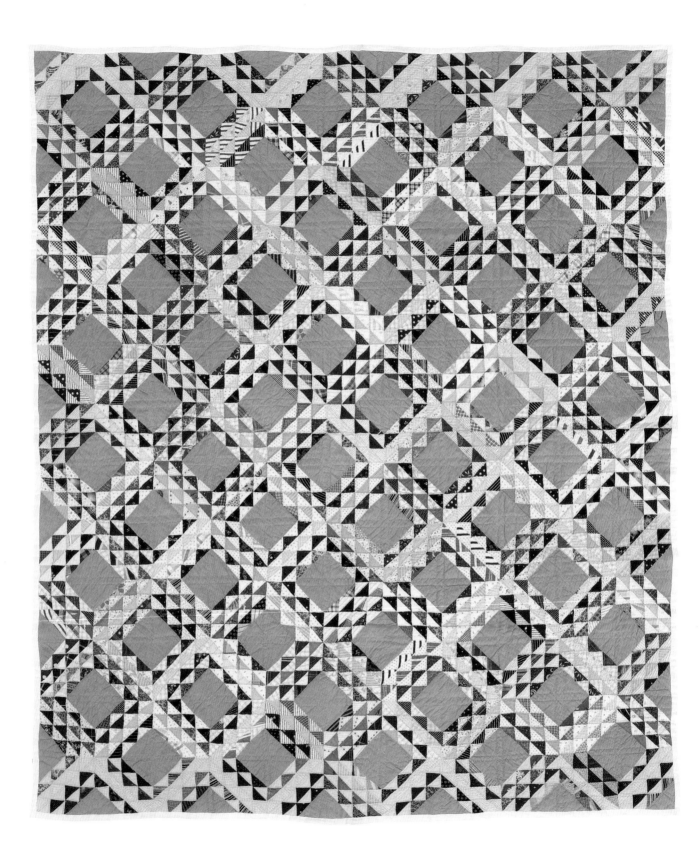

From one pink print, cut:
- 10—2⅜" squares
- 2—2⅜" squares, cutting each in half diagonally for 4 triangles total

From *each* of two medium or dark prints, cut:
- 3—2⅜" squares

From a third medium or dark print, cut:
- 4—2⅜" squares

From a fourth medium or dark print, cut:
- 2—2⅜" squares, cutting each in half diagonally for 4 triangles total

1. Use a pencil to mark a diagonal line on wrong side of each pink print 2⅜" square.

2. Layer each marked pink print square atop a medium or dark print 2⅜" square. Sew each pair together with two seams, stitching ¼" on each side of drawn line (**Diagram 1**).

3. Cut a pair apart on drawn line to make two triangle units (**Diagram 2**). Press open each triangle unit to make two pink triangle-squares (**Diagram 3**). Each triangle-square should be 2" square including seam allowances. Repeat to make 20 triangle-squares total.

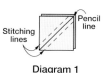
Stitching lines

Pencil line

Diagram 1

Diagram 2

Diagram 3

4. Referring to **Diagram 4**, lay out 10 pink triangle-squares (three each from first and second prints, and four from the third print), two pink print triangles, and two medium or dark print triangles in four rows.

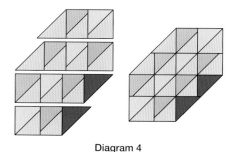
Diagram 4

5. Sew together pieces in each row. Press seams in one direction, alternating direction with each row. Join rows to make a pink Ocean Waves unit. Press seams in one direction.

6. Repeat steps 4 and 5 to make a second pink Ocean Waves unit.

Light Ocean Waves Units
Substituting a light print for the pink print and referring to **Diagram 5**, repeat cutting and assembly instructions for Pink Ocean Waves Units, *page 31*, to make 120 light Ocean Waves units total (you will use 119).

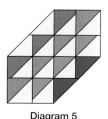
Diagram 5

Assemble Quilt Top

To piece the quilt top, you will first make diagonal rows that include the inset angles for joining rows. As you follow these steps, refer to **Quilt Assembly Diagram** and **Diagrams 6 and 7** to view the construction of each row. You will then join the rows with set-in seams. (For details, see Set In Pieces, *page 158*.)

1. Referring to **Quilt Assembly Diagram** on *page 34*, lay out pink Ocean Waves units, light Ocean Waves units, solid blue setting squares, and solid blue setting triangles in 11 diagonal rows. Note placement of medium or dark print triangles in triangle-squares.

2. Referring to **Diagram 6**, pick up first diagonal row's setting pieces and Ocean Waves units between setting pieces. Join pieces, making sure you don't stitch into ¼" seam allowances. Press all seams toward Ocean Waves units.

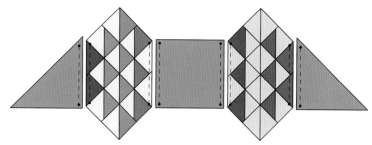
Diagram 6

continued

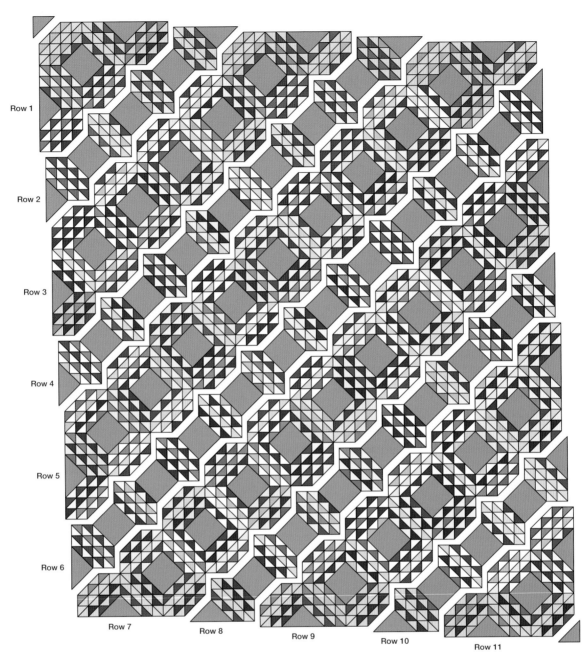

Row 1
Row 2
Row 3
Row 4
Row 5
Row 6
Row 7
Row 8
Row 9
Row 10
Row 11

Quilt Assembly Diagram

3. To set in remaining Ocean Waves units in first row, pin one diagonal edge of an Ocean Waves unit to diagonal edge of Ocean Waves unit at beginning of row (**Diagram 7**). Sew from inside seam to outside corner, making sure you don't sew into $\frac{1}{4}$" seam allowance. Bring up setting square and pin it to Ocean Waves unit; stitch together. Pin diagonal edge of adjacent Ocean Waves unit in the row to the unit being added. Sew from inside seam to outside corner. Press seams away from unit just added.

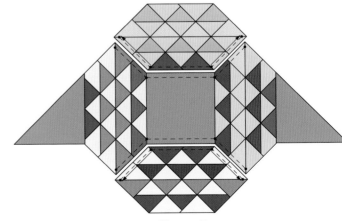

Diagram 7

4. Repeat Step 3 to set in an Ocean Waves unit on opposite side of row to complete a wide Ocean Waves row (**Diagram 7**).

5. Repeat steps 2–4 with odd-numbered diagonal rows to make six wide Ocean Waves rows total.

6. Repeat Step 2 with even-numbered diagonal rows to make five narrow Ocean Waves rows total.

7. Join wide and narrow rows by setting in Ocean Waves units as before. Make sure you don't sew into ¼" seam allowances. Press seams toward narrow Ocean Waves rows.

8. Add two solid blue corner triangles to complete quilt top. Press seams toward corner triangles.

Finish Quilt

1. Layer quilt top, batting, and backing; baste. (For details, see Complete Quilt, *page 159.*)

2. Quilt as desired. The quilter of this antique piece hand-quilted ⅛" inside each triangle. In the setting squares and triangles, she stitched a cross motif (**Quilting Diagram**).

3. Bind with solid white binding strips. (For details, see Complete Quilt.)

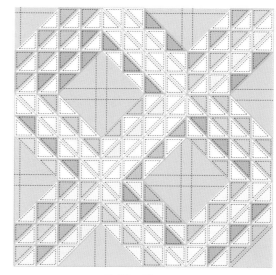

Quilting Diagram

optional colors

Golden Glow

For this 40×28" version of *Making Waves,* quilt tester Laura Boehnke arranged six assembled Ocean Waves X-shape units three across and two deep. A 2"-wide-finished navy blue border sets off the wall hanging. The richly colored palette, accented with warm gold, is a choice with masculine appeal.

TOILE TABLE RUNNER

A single row of Ocean Waves octagon units gets a classic two-color treatment.

Materials

1⅜ yards red-and-cream toile (blocks)

¾ yard total assorted red prints (blocks)

⅜ yard red-and-black print (binding)

1 yard backing fabric

20×71" batting

Finished table runner: 13¼×64¼"

Cut Fabrics

Cut pieces in the following order.

From red-and-cream toile, cut:
- 2—9¾" squares, cutting each diagonally twice in an X for 8 setting triangles total
- 2—5⅛" squares, cutting each in half diagonally for 4 corner triangles total
- 5—4¾" squares
- 100—2⅜" squares
- 20—2⅜" squares, cutting each in half diagonally for 40 triangles total

From assorted red prints, cut:
- 100—2⅜" squares
- 20—2⅜" squares, cutting each in half diagonally for 40 triangles total

From red-and-black print, cut:
- 4—2½×42" binding strips

Assemble Ocean Waves Units

1. Use a pencil to mark a diagonal line on wrong side of each red-and-cream toile 2⅜" square.

2. Referring to Cut and Assemble Ocean Waves Units, steps 2 and 3, *page 33,* use marked red-and-cream toile squares and assorted red print 2⅜" squares to make 200 triangle-squares total.

3. Referring to Cut and Assemble Ocean Waves Units, steps 4 and 5, use 10 triangle-squares, two red-and-cream toile triangles, and two assorted red print triangles to make an Ocean Waves unit (**Diagram 8**). Repeat to make 20 Ocean Waves units total.

Assemble Table Runner Top

1. Referring to **Diagram 9**, lay out two Ocean Waves units and one red-and-cream toile 4¾" square in a horizontal row. Join pieces, making sure you don't stitch into ¼" seam allowances. Press seams toward Ocean Waves units.

2. Referring to Assemble Quilt Top, Step 3, *page 34,* set Ocean Waves units into remaining edges of red-and-cream toile square to make an octagon unit (**Diagram 9**; note placement of red prints in units).

3. Repeat steps 1 and 2 to make five octagon units total.

4. Referring to **Table Runner Assembly Diagram**, lay out octagon units in a vertical row, rotating every other block as shown. Join blocks, making sure you don't stitch into ¼" seam allowances. Press seams in one direction.

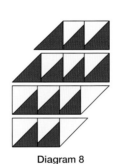

Diagram 8

Diagram 9

Table Runner
Assembly Diagram

5. Referring to **Table Runner Assembly Diagram,** *page 37,* set in red-and-cream toile setting triangles. Add red-and-cream toile corner triangles to complete table runner top. Press all seams toward triangles.

Finish Table Runner

1. Layer table runner top, batting, and backing; baste. (For details, see Complete Quilt, *page 159.*) Quilt as desired.

2. Bind with red-and-black print binding strips. (For details, see Complete Quilt.)

FRAMED PHOTO BLOCK

Preserve a special photo—on fabric!

Materials

¼ yard total assorted cream-and-tan prints (block)

⅛ yard total assorted tan prints (block)

9×22" piece (fat eighth) solid black (block)

16" square lining fabric

16" square thin batting

1 sheet printer fabric

Photo (image will be trimmed to 4¾" square)

Frame with 12" square opening

Finished wall hanging (inside opening): 12" square

Cut Fabrics

Cut pieces in the following order.

From assorted cream-and-tan prints, cut:
* 20—2⅜" squares
* 4—2⅜" squares, cutting each in half diagonally for 8 triangles total

From assorted tan prints, cut:
* 20—2⅜" squares
* 4—2⅜" squares, cutting each in half diagonally for 8 triangles total

From solid black, cut:
* 2—5⅛" squares, cutting each in half diagonally for 4 corner triangles total

Assemble Ocean Waves Units

1. Use a pencil to mark a diagonal line on wrong side of each assorted cream-and-tan print 2⅜" square.

2. Referring to Cut and Assemble Ocean Waves Units, steps 2 and 3, *page 33,* use marked cream-and-tan print squares and assorted tan print 2⅜" squares to make 40 triangle-squares total.

3. Referring to Cut and Assemble Ocean Waves Units, steps 4 and 5, use 10 triangle-squares, two assorted cream-and-tan print triangles, and two assorted tan print triangles to make an Ocean Waves unit **(Diagram 10).** Repeat to make four Ocean Waves units total.

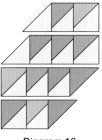

Diagram 10

Assemble Block

1. Following manufacturer's instructions, print desired photo onto printer fabric. Trim fabric photo to 4¾" square including seam allowances.

2. Referring to **Diagram 11**, lay out two Ocean Waves units and fabric photo square in a horizontal row. Join pieces, making sure you don't stitch into ¼" seam allowances. Press seams toward Ocean Waves units.

Diagram 11

3. Referring to Assemble Quilt Top, Step 3, *page 34,* set Ocean Waves units into remaining edges of fabric photo square (**Diagram 11**).

4. Add solid black corner triangles to make a block. Press seams toward triangles. The block should be 13¼" square including seam allowances.

Finish Wall Hanging

1. Layer block, batting, and lining; baste. (For details, see Complete Quilt, *page 159.*)

2. Quilt as desired. This block is stitched in the ditch around each triangle.

3. Centering fabric photo, trim quilted block to same size as cardboard in frame. Zigzag-stitch around all edges to secure layers and prevent fraying.

4. Mount and insert block into frame.

CRAZY ABOUT COLOR

A pattern gives a quilt a solid foundation, but colors
give it a personality all its own. From high-contrast
combos to monochromatic palettes, the eye-catching
examples in this chapter prove the options are endless.
Gain the confidence you need to breathe life into
your quilts by experimenting with pairings, saturation,
and intensity.

62

52

66

42

BOHEMIAN *Charm*

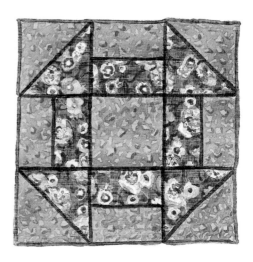

Transform your bedroom with funky fabrics and rotary-cut blocks in four sizes

for this bed quilt from designers Sarah Maxwell and Dolores Smith.

Materials

5⅔ yards total assorted tone-on-tones in orange, fuchsia, red, gold, green, purple, blue, turquoise, and brown (blocks)

4⅞ yards total assorted prints in orange, fuchsia, red, green, purple, blue, turquoise, and brown (blocks)

¾ yard turquoise tone-on-tone (binding)

7⅛ yards backing fabric

85×103" batting

Finished quilt: 78½×96½"
Finished blocks: 16", 10", 6", and 4" square

Quantities are for 44/45" wide, 100% cotton fabrics. **Measurements** include ¼" seam allowances. Sew with right sides together unless otherwise stated.

Designer Notes

As quilt shop owners, designers Sarah Maxwell and Dolores Smith feel lucky to be able to see the latest fabric lines, such as these vibrant prints, before they hit store shelves. "We simply loved this collection, so we designed a quilt to showcase it," Sarah says. With four sizes of Churn Dash blocks in the double-bed-size quilt, Sarah and Dolores were able to feature each of the different-size prints to their best advantage. "Although the quilt is multicolored, it's made cohesive by using all tone-on-tone prints in the block backgrounds," Dolores says.

Cut Fabrics

Cut pieces in the following order. Cut each set of pieces from matching fabric.

From assorted tone-on-tones, cut:
- 16 sets of one 3⅛×25" strip, two 6⅛" squares, and one 6" square
- 18 sets of one 2⅛×17" strip, two 4⅛" squares, and one 4" square
- 26 sets of one 1½×11" strip, two 2⅞" squares, and one 2½" square
- 29 sets of one 1⅛×9" strip, two 2⅛" squares, and one 2" square

From assorted prints, cut:
- 16 sets of one 3⅛×25" strip and two 6⅛" squares
- 18 sets of one 2⅛×17" strip and two 4⅛" squares
- 26 sets of one 1½×11" strip and two 2⅞" squares
- 29 sets of one 1⅛×9" strip and two 2⅛" squares
- 48—2½" squares

From turquoise tone-on-tone, cut:
- 9—2½×42" binding strips

Assemble Blocks

1. For a large Churn Dash block, you'll need a set of matching tone-on-tone pieces (one 3⅛×25" strip, two 6⅛" squares, and one 6" square) and a set of matching print pieces (one 3⅛×25" strip and two 6⅛" squares).

continued

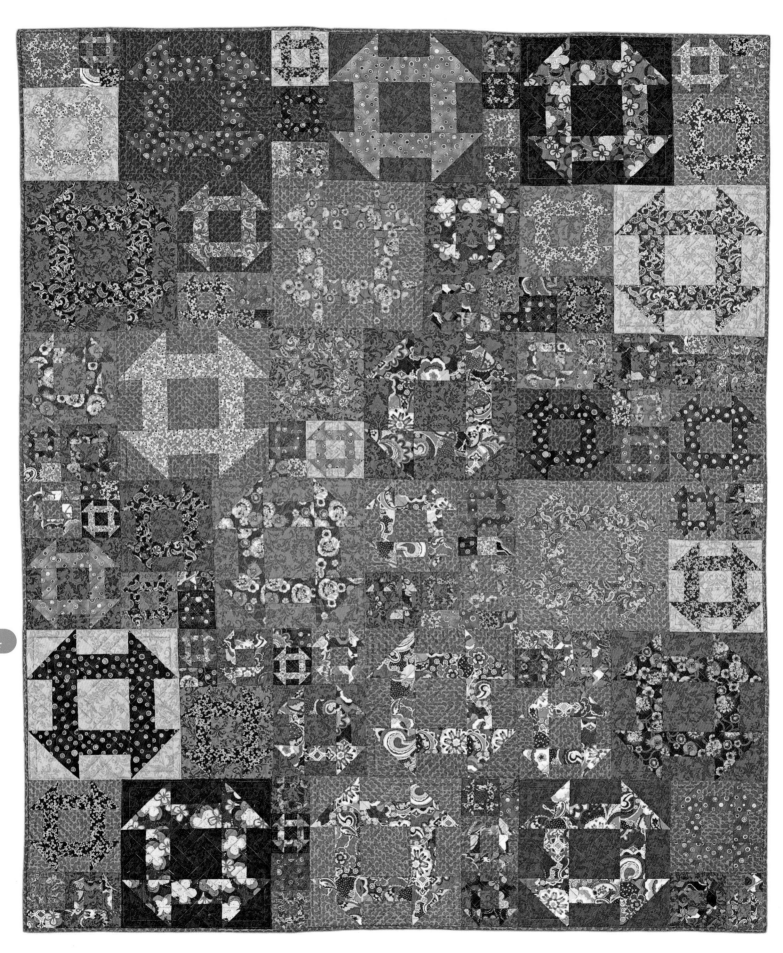

Bohemian Charm

2. Use a pencil to mark a diagonal line on wrong side of each tone-on-tone 6⅛" square.

3. Layer a marked tone-on-tone square atop each print 6⅛" square. Sew each pair together with two seams, stitching ¼" on each side of drawn line **(Diagram 1)**. Cut each pair apart on drawn line to make two triangle units. Press each triangle unit open, pressing seam toward darker fabric, to make four triangle-squares total. Each triangle-square should be 5¾" square including seam allowances.

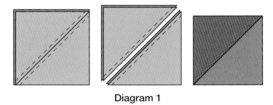

Diagram 1

4. Join a tone-on-tone 3⅛×25" strip and a print 3⅛×25" strip to make a strip set **(Diagram 2)**. Press seam toward darker fabric. Cut strip set into four 6"-wide segments. Each segment should be 5¾×6" including seam allowances.

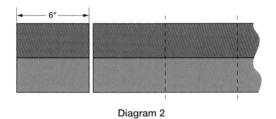

Diagram 2

5. Referring to **Diagram 3**, lay out four triangle-squares, four 6"-wide segments, and a tone-on-tone 6" square in three rows. Sew together pieces in each row. Press seams toward 6"-wide segments. Join

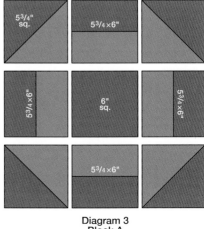

Diagram 3
Block A

rows to make Churn Dash Block A. Press seams in one direction. The block should be 16½" square including seam allowances.

6. Repeat steps 1–5 to make 16 total of Churn Dash Block A.

7. For one Churn Dash Block B, gather a set of matching tone-on-tone pieces (one 2⅛×17" strip, two 4⅛" squares, and one 4" square) and a set of matching print pieces (one 2⅛×17" strip and two 4⅛" squares). Using 4⅛" squares, repeat steps 2 and 3 to make four triangle-squares. Each triangle-square should be 3¾" square including seam allowances. Using 2⅛×17" strips and referring to **Diagram 4**, repeat Step 4 to make four 4"-wide segments. Each segment should be 3¾×4" including seam allowances. Referring to **Diagram 5**, repeat Step 5 to make Churn Dash Block B. The block should be 10½" square including seam allowances. Repeat to make 18 total of Churn Dash Block B.

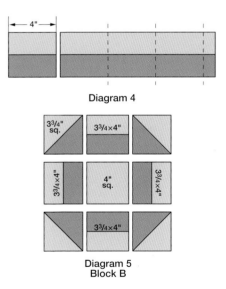

Diagram 4

Diagram 5
Block B

8. For one Churn Dash Block C, gather a set of matching tone-on-tone pieces (one 1½×11" strip, two 2⅞" squares, and one 2½" square) and a set of matching print pieces (one 1½×11" strip and two 2⅞" squares). Using 2⅞" squares, repeat steps 2 and 3 to make four triangle-squares. Each triangle-square should be 2½" square including seam allowances. Using 1½×11" strips and referring to **Diagram 6**,

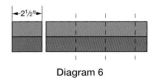

Diagram 6

continued

Bohemian Charm

Quilt Assembly Diagram

repeat Step 4 to make four 2½"-wide segments. Each segment should be 2½" square including seam allowances. Referring to **Diagram 7**, repeat Step 5 to make Churn Dash Block C. The block should be 6½" square including seam allowances. Repeat to make 26 total of Churn Dash Block C.

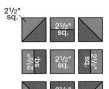

Diagram 7
Block C

9. For one Churn Dash Block D, gather a set of matching tone-on-tone pieces (one 1⅛×9" strip, two 2⅛" squares, and one 2" square) and a set of matching print pieces (one 1⅛×9" strip and two 2⅛" squares). Using 2⅛" squares, repeat steps 2 and 3 to make four triangle-squares. Each triangle-square should be 1¾" square including seam allowances. Using 1⅛×9" strips and referring to **Diagram 8**, repeat Step 4 to make four 2"-wide segments. Each segment should be 1¾×2" including seam allowances. Referring to **Diagram 9**, repeat Step 5 to make Churn Dash Block D. The block should be 4½" square including seam allowances. Repeat to make 29 total of Churn Dash Block D.

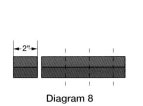

Diagram 8

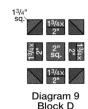

Diagram 9
Block D

Assemble Quilt Top

1. Referring to **Quilt Assembly Diagram**, lay out Churn Dash blocks A–D and assorted print 2½" squares in 19 sections (all horizontal rows have three sections except row four, which has four sections).

2. To join pieces in each section, first sew together the 2½" squares; press seams in one direction. Add joined squares to Churn Dash D blocks; press seams toward blocks. Continue adding next-largest blocks to complete each section.

3. Sew together sections in each horizontal row. Press seams in one direction, alternating direction with each row. Join rows to complete quilt top. Press seams in one direction.

Finish Quilt

1. Layer quilt top, batting, and backing; baste. (For details, see Complete Quilt, *page 159.*)

2. Quilt as desired. Machine-quilter Connie Gresham stitched a Celtic knot design in each Churn Dash block.

3. Bind with turquoise tone-on-tone binding strips. (For details, see Complete Quilt.)

optional colors

Push and Pull

When she saw the variety of colors and values in this floral collection, quilt tester Laura Boehnke decided to do a study in contrast. The result? A romantic wall hanging whose four sizes of Churn Dash blocks are further differentiated by how much or how little their fabrics contrast. Laura added a 1¾"-wide-finished border to frame the piece.

TONE-ON-TONE TABLE RUNNER

Create clean, crisp Churn Dash blocks with subtle prints.

Materials

$1\frac{7}{8}$ yards total assorted cream prints and tone-
   on-tones in orange, peach, yellow, green,
   light green, light blue, and lavender (blocks)

$\frac{1}{2}$ yard lavender tone-on-tone (binding)

$1\frac{1}{3}$ yards backing fabric

23×71" batting

Finished table runner: $16\frac{1}{2}×64\frac{1}{2}$"

Cut Fabrics

Cut pieces in the following order. Cut each set of pieces from matching fabric.

From assorted cream prints and tone-on-tones, cut:
- 2 sets of one $3\frac{1}{8}×25$" strip, two $6\frac{1}{8}$" squares, and one 6" square
- 2 sets of one $3\frac{1}{8}×25$" strip and two $6\frac{1}{8}$" squares
- 2 sets of one $2\frac{1}{8}×17$" strip, two $4\frac{1}{8}$" squares, and one 4" square
- 2 sets of one $2\frac{1}{8}×17$" strip and two $4\frac{1}{8}$" squares
- 6 sets of one $1\frac{1}{2}×11$" strip, two $2\frac{7}{8}$" squares, and one $2\frac{1}{2}$" square
- 6 sets of one $1\frac{1}{2}×11$" strip and two $2\frac{7}{8}$" squares
- 4 sets of one $1\frac{1}{8}×9$" strip, two $2\frac{1}{8}$" squares, and one 2" square
- 4 sets of one $1\frac{1}{8}×9$" strip and two $2\frac{1}{8}$" squares

From remaining assorted tone-on-tones, cut:
- 8—$2\frac{1}{2}$" squares

From lavender tone-on-tone, cut:
- 5—$2\frac{1}{2}×42$" binding strips

Assemble Blocks

1. Referring to Assemble Blocks, steps 2–5, *page 45*, use a set of one $3\frac{1}{8}×25$" strip, two $6\frac{1}{8}$" squares, and one 6" square; and a contrasting set of one $3\frac{1}{8}×25$" strip and two $6\frac{1}{8}$" squares to make Churn Dash Block A. Repeat to make a second Churn Dash Block A.

2. Referring to Assemble Blocks, Step 7, use a set of one $2\frac{1}{8}×17$" strip, two $4\frac{1}{8}$" squares, and one 4" square; and a contrasting set of one $2\frac{1}{8}×17$" strip and two $4\frac{1}{8}$" squares to make Churn Dash Block B. Repeat to make a second Churn Dash Block B.

3. Referring to Assemble Blocks, Step 8, use a set of one $1\frac{1}{2}×11$" strip, two $2\frac{7}{8}$" squares, and one $2\frac{1}{2}$" square; and a contrasting set of one $1\frac{1}{2}×11$" strip and two $2\frac{7}{8}$" squares to make Churn Dash Block C. Repeat to make six total of Churn Dash Block C.

4. Referring to Assemble Blocks, Step 9, *page 47*, use a set of one $1\frac{1}{8}×9$" strip, two $2\frac{1}{8}$" squares, and one 2" square; and a set of one $1\frac{1}{8}×9$" strip and two $2\frac{1}{8}$" squares to make Churn Dash Block D. Repeat to make four total of Churn Dash Block D.

Assemble Table Runner Top

1. Referring to **Table Runner Assembly Diagram**, lay out blocks and assorted tone-on-tone $2\frac{1}{2}$" squares in six sections.

2. Referring to Assemble Quilt Top, Step 2, *page 47*, join pieces in each section.

3. Sew together sections to complete table runner top. Press seams in one direction.

Finish Table Runner

1. Layer table runner top, batting, and backing; baste. (For details, see Complete Quilt, *page 159*.)

2. Quilt as desired. This table runner is quilted with sections of parallel zigzag lines running vertically, horizontally, and diagonally.

3. Bind with lavender tone-on-tone binding strips. (For details, see Complete Quilt.)

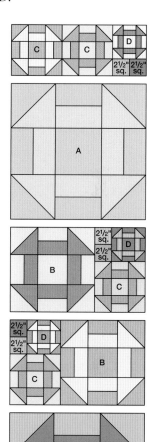

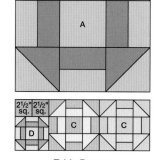

Table Runner
Assembly Diagram

CHECKERBOARD THROW

Use Churn Dash blocks in just one size and create contrast with light, medium, and dark batiks.

Materials

1½ yards total assorted light to medium batiks (blocks)

1½ yards total assorted dark batiks (blocks)

1¼ yards tan batik (setting squares)

⅓ yard rust batik (inner border)

1¾ yards black batik (outer border, binding)

3⅞ yards backing fabric

68" square batting

Finished quilt: 61½" square

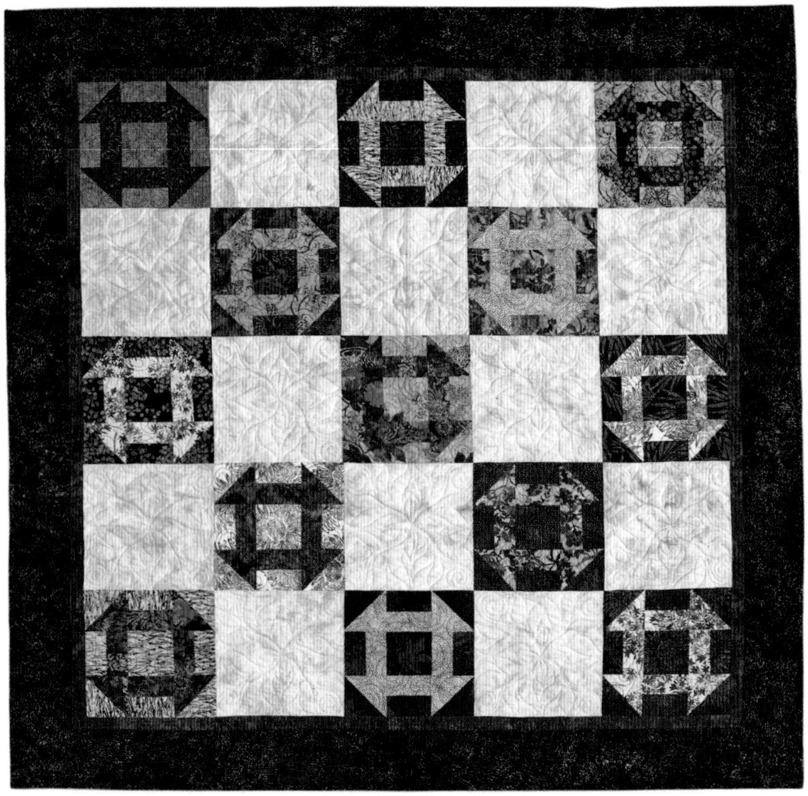

Cut Fabrics

Cut pieces in the order that follows. Cut each set of pieces from matching fabric.

From assorted light and medium batiks, cut:
- 8 sets of one 2⅛×17" strip and two 4⅛" squares
- 5 sets of one 2⅛×17" strip, two 4⅛" squares, and one 4" square

From assorted dark batiks, cut:
- 8 sets of one 2⅛×17" strip, two 4⅛" squares, and one 4" square
- 5 sets of one 2⅛×17" strip and two 4⅛" squares

From tan batik, cut:
- 12—10½" setting squares

From rust batik, cut:
- 6—1½×42" strips for inner border

From black batik, cut:
- 7—5×42" strips for outer border
- 67—2½×42" binding strips

Assemble Blocks

1. Referring to Assemble Blocks, Step 7, *page 45,* use a light or medium batik set of one 2⅛×17" strip, two 4⅛" squares, and one 4" square; and a dark batik set of one 2⅛×17" strip and two 4⅛" squares to make dark Churn Dash Block B **(Diagram 10).** Repeat to make five total of dark Churn Dash Block B.

2. Referring to Assemble Blocks, Step 7, use a dark batik set of one 2⅛×17" strip, two 4⅛" squares, and one 4" square; and a light or medium batik set of one 2⅛×17" strip and two 4⅛" squares to make light Churn Dash Block B **(Diagram 11).** Repeat to make eight total of light Churn Dash Block B.

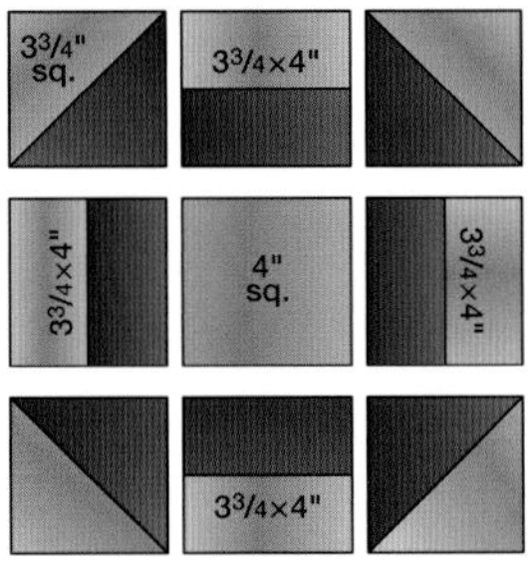

Diagram 10

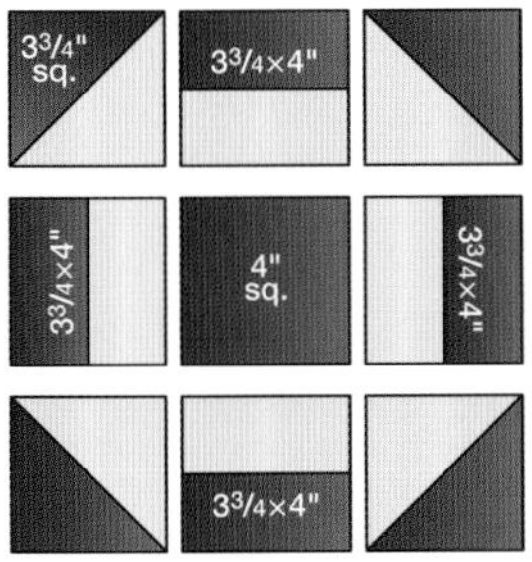

Diagram 11

Assemble Quilt Center

1. Referring to photo *opposite,* lay out blocks and tan batik setting squares in five rows, positioning dark Churn Dash blocks and light Churn Dash blocks as desired. Sew together pieces in each row. Press seams toward setting squares.

2. Join rows to make quilt center. Press seams in one direction. The quilt center should be 50½" square including seam allowances.

Add Borders

1. Cut and piece rust batik 1½×42" strips to make:
- 2—1½×52½" inner border strips
- 2—1½×50½" inner border strips

2. Sew short inner border strips to opposite edges of quilt center. Add long inner border strips to remaining edges. Press all seams toward inner border.

3. Cut and piece black batik 5×42" strips to make:
- 2—5×61½" outer border strips
- 2—5×52½" outer border strips

4. Sew short outer border strips to opposite edges of quilt center. Add long outer border strips to remaining edges to complete quilt top. Press all seams toward outer border.

Finish Quilt

1. Layer quilt top, batting, and backing; baste. (For details, see Complete Quilt, *page 159.*)

2. Quilt as desired. Each setting square in this quilt features a stylized floral motif; spiral designs are quilted in the blocks and borders.

3. Bind with black batik binding strips. (For details, see Complete Quilt.)

Crossroads

Stand back and see how the blocks create intersecting paths on designer

Marti Michell's lively variation of a classic design.

Materials

½ yard dark red print (blocks)

2—¼-yard pieces assorted gold prints (blocks)

1⅓ yards mottled orange (blocks)

1¼ yards total assorted bright prints (blocks)

⅓ yard hand-dyed green (inner border)

1½ yards red floral (outer border, binding)

3¾ yards backing fabric

67" square batting

Finished quilt: 60½" square
Finished block: 12" square

Quantities are for 44/45"-wide, 100% cotton fabrics.
Measurements include ¼" seam allowances. Sew with right sides together unless otherwise stated.

Size options: For a chart of optional sizes, turn to *Pattern Sheet 1.*

Cut Fabrics

Cut pieces in the following order.

From dark red print, cut:
- 32—3½" squares

From *each* gold print, cut:
- 16—3½" squares

From mottled orange, cut:
- 32—6½" squares (In the featured quilt, designer Marti Michell used a directional, woven ikat fabric. If you're using a similar fabric, cut squares on the bias.)

From assorted bright prints, cut:
- 128—3½" squares

From hand-dyed green, cut:
- 5—2×42" strips for inner border

From red floral, cut:
- 6—5×42" strips for outer border
- 7—2½×42" binding strips

Assemble Blocks

1. Mark a diagonal line on wrong side of each dark red print and gold print 3½" square.

2. Align a marked dark red print 3½" square with one corner of a mottled orange 6½" square (**Diagram 1** on *page 54;* note direction of drawn line). Sew on drawn line; trim excess, leaving ¼" seam allowance. Press open attached triangle.

continued

3. Align a marked gold print 3½" square with opposite corner of mottled orange square (**Diagram 1**; again note direction of drawn line). Stitch, trim, and press as before to make a Floating Star unit. The unit should be 6½" square including seam allowances.

Diagram 1

4. Repeat steps 2 and 3 to make 32 Floating Star units total.

5. Sew together four assorted bright print 3½" squares in pairs (**Diagram 2**). Press seams in opposite directions. Join pairs to make a Four-Patch unit. Press seam in one direction. The unit should be 6½" square including seam allowances. Repeat to make 32 Four-Patch units total.

Diagram 2

6. Referring to **Diagram 3**, sew together two Four-Patch units and two Floating Star units in pairs. Press seams in opposite directions. Join pairs to make an Arkansas Crossroads block. Press seam in

one direction. The block should be 12½" square including seam allowances. Repeat to make 16 Arkansas Crossroads blocks total.

Assemble Quilt Top

1. Referring to **Quilt Assembly Diagram**, lay out blocks in rows, noting direction of Floating Star units and placement of gold prints.

2. Sew together blocks in each row. Press seams in one direction, alternating direction with each row.

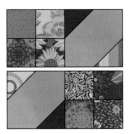

Diagram 3

continued

Quilt Assembly Diagram

3. Join rows to make quilt center. Press seams in one direction. The quilt center should be 48½" square including seam allowances.

4. Cut and piece hand-dyed green 2×42" strips to make:
- 2—2×51½" inner border strips
- 2—2×48½" inner border strips

5. Sew short inner border strips to opposite edges of quilt center. Add long inner border strips to remaining edges. Press all seams toward inner border.

6. Cut and piece red floral 5×42" strips to make:
- 2—5×60½" outer border strips
- 2—5×51½" outer border strips

7. Sew short outer border strips to opposite edges of quilt center. Add long outer border strips to remaining edges to complete quilt top. Press all seams toward outer border.

Finish Quilt

1. Layer quilt top, batting, and backing; baste. (For details, see Complete Quilt, *page 159.*)

2. Quilt as desired. In each block, Marti machine-quilted parallel lines from corner to corner in the mottled orange and stitched in the ditch around the squares.

3. Bind with red floral binding strips. (For details, see Complete Quilt.)

optional colors

Four Corners

Make a quick wall hanging version of *Crossroads* as quilt tester Laura Boehnke did using harmonizing prints in turquoise and brown. With just four Arkansas Crossroads blocks, attention goes right to the medallion shape formed where the blocks meet.

Although the prints in the Four-Patch units vary in color, value, and scale, they're all set off well by the same chocolate brown tone-on-tone used as the base of each Floating Star unit.

CROSSWAYS QUILT

Create one-way movement instead of intersecting paths by arranging Four-Patch units and setting squares in a diagonal Irish Chain pattern.

Materials

1½ yards total assorted dark blue prints
(Four-Patch units, binding)

1½ yards total assorted medium blue prints and
stripes (Four-Patch units, binding)

1 yard medium blue floral (Four-Patch units,
binding)

¾ yard light blue print (Four-Patch units)

2¾ yards white-and-blue print (setting squares)

⅔ yard dark blue floral (inner border)

1½ yards blue-and-white floral (outer border)

8⅛ yards backing fabric

97" square batting

Finished quilt: 90½" square

Cut Fabrics

Cut pieces in the
following order.

From assorted dark blue
prints, cut:
• 7—2½×22" strips
  for binding
• 112—3½" squares
  (56 sets of 2
  matching squares)
From assorted medium
blue prints and stripes, cut:
• 7—2½×22" strips for
  binding
• 112—3½" squares
  (56 sets of 2
  matching squares)

From medium blue floral, cut:
• 5—2½×22" strips for binding
• 58—3½" squares
From light blue print, cut:
• 58—3½" squares
From white-and-blue print, cut:
• 84—6½" setting squares
From dark blue floral, cut:
• 9—2½×42" strips for inner border
From blue-and-white floral, cut:
• 10—4½×42" strips for outer border

Assemble Quilt Center

1. Referring to Assemble Blocks, Step 5, *page 54,* use
two matching dark blue print 3½" squares and two
matching medium blue print or stripe 3½" squares
to make a dark Four-Patch unit **(Diagram 4)**. Repeat
to make 56 dark Four-Patch units total.

2. Using two medium blue floral 3½" squares and
two light blue print 3½" squares, repeat Step 1 to
make 29 light Four-Patch units **(Diagram 5)**.

| Diagram 4 | Diagram 5 |

3. Referring to photo, *opposite,* lay out Four-Patch units and white-and-blue print setting squares in 13 rows. In the lower right portion of the featured quilt, rows of dark and light Four-Patch units alternate, creating diagonal bands of similar colors. The upper left portion contains more dark units than light units and has a less structured color pattern.

4. Sew together pieces in each row. Press seams toward setting squares. Join rows to make quilt center. Press seams in one direction. The quilt center should be 78½" square including seam allowances.

Add Borders

1. Cut and piece dark blue floral 2½×42" strips to make:
- 2—2½×82½" inner border strips
- 2—2½×78½" inner border strips

2. Sew short inner border strips to opposite edges of quilt center. Add long inner border strips to remaining edges. Press all seams toward inner border.

3. Cut and piece blue-and-white floral 4½×42" strips to make:
- 2—4½×90½" outer border strips
- 2—4½×82½" outer border strips

4. Sew short outer border strips to opposite edges of quilt center. Add long outer border strips to remaining edges to complete quilt top. Press all seams toward outer border.

Finish Quilt

1. Layer quilt top, batting, and backing; baste. (For details, see Complete Quilt, *page 159.*)

2. Quilt as desired. The featured quilt was stitched with an allover feather design.

3. Using diagonal seams, join assorted dark blue print, assorted medium blue print, and medium blue floral 2½×22" strips to make a pieced binding strip. Bind with pieced binding strip. (For details, see Complete Quilt.)

PILLOW PAIR

Join four almost identical units to make complementary pillow covers.

Materials for two pillows

1¾ yards tan print (pillow center, border, pillow

backs, covered button)

⅛ yard *each* purple floral and purple stripe (pillow

centers)

Scraps of purple dot and purple herringbone print

(pillow center)

½ yard dark green print (pillow center, border,

covered button)

⅛ yard light green print (pillow center)

2—24" squares flannel (lining)

2—1½"-diameter buttons to cover

2—¾"-diameter buttons

2—12"-square pillow forms

Dollmaker's needle

Heavy-duty thread

Finished pillows: 19" square

continued

Cut Fabrics

Cut pieces in the following order.

From tan print, cut:
* 4—19½×23½" rectangles
* 4—4×20½" border strips
* 4—6½" squares
* 1—2¼" square

From *each* of purple floral and purple stripe, cut:
* 6—3½" squares

From *each* of purple dot and purple herringbone, cut:
* 2—3½" squares

From dark green print, cut:
* 4—4×20½" border strips
* 4—3½" squares
* 1—2¼" square

From light green print, cut:
* 4—3½" squares

Assemble Floating Star Pillow Cover

1. Referring to Assemble Blocks, steps 2 and 3, *pages 53 and 54,* and photo, *below left,* use tan print 6½" squares and two each of purple floral, stripe, dot, and herringbone print 3½" squares to make four Floating Star units.

2. Referring to photo, *below left,* sew together Floating Star units in pairs. Press seams in opposite directions. Join pairs to make pillow center. Press seam in one direction. The pillow center should be 12½" square including seam allowances.

3. With midpoints aligned, sew dark green print border strips to opposite edges of pillow center, beginning and ending seams ¼" from corners. Add dark green print border strips to remaining edges, mitering corners, to complete pillow top. (For details, see Miter Borders, *page 158.*) The pillow top should be 19½" square including seam allowances.

4. Layer a flannel 24" lining square atop wrong side of pillow top; baste. Quilt as desired. The featured pillow is quilted with diagonal grid lines. Trim flannel lining even with pillow top edges.

5. With wrong side inside, fold two tan print 19½×23½" rectangles in half to make two 11¾×19½" double-thick pillow back rectangles. Overlap folded edges by about 4" to make a 19½"-square pillow back **(Diagram 6)**. Baste along top and bottom edges to secure pieces.

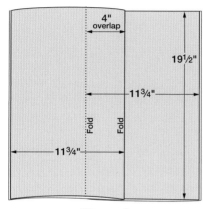

Diagram 6

6. With right sides together, layer quilted pillow top and pillow back; pin or baste edges. Sew together through all layers. Turn right side out through opening in pillow back. Stitch in the ditch along border seam, backstitching at each overlap on pillow back, to create a flange and make Floating Star pillow cover.

Assemble Four-Patch Pillow Cover

1. Referring to Assemble Blocks, Step 5, *page 54,* use two light green print 3½" squares, one purple floral 3½" square, and one purple stripe 3½" square to make a light green Four-Patch unit **(Diagram 7)**. Repeat to make a second light green Four-Patch unit.

2. Repeat Step 1, substituting dark green print 3½" squares for light green print squares, to make two dark green Four-Patch units **(Diagram 8)**.

Diagram 7

Diagram 8

3. Referring to photo, *opposite, below right,* join light green and dark green Four-Patch units in pairs. Press seams in opposite directions. Join pairs to make pillow center. Press seam in one direction. The pillow center should be 12½" square including seam allowances.

4. Referring to Assemble Floating Star Pillow Cover, Step 3, use tan print border strips to make pillow top.

5. Referring to Assemble Floating Star Pillow Cover, steps 4–6, quilt pillow top and add pillow back to make Four-Patch pillow cover.

Add Buttons

1. Following manufacturer's instructions, cover 1½"-diameter buttons using dark green print and tan print 2¼" squares.

2. Insert a 12"-square pillow form in Floating Star pillow cover. Thread and knot a dollmaker's needle with heavy-duty thread, leaving an 8" tail beyond knot. Holding pillow back open, push needle through center of pillow form to center of pillow top. Attach dark green print covered button, and push needle back through pillow form. Attach a ¾"-diameter button at the center back of pillow form, and pull thread taut. Repeat to stitch once more through both buttons. Knot thread ends at base of ¾"-diameter button to complete pillow cover.

3. Using tan print covered button, repeat Step 2 to add buttons to Four-Patch pillow cover.

Zen

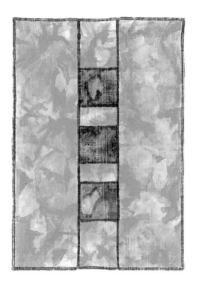

The cool colors and organic motifs of batiks give designer Amy Walsh's contemporary throw a calming vibe. Horizontal rows of stitches flow like rivers across the quilt, adding to its serene feeling.

Materials

5 yards total assorted blue and blue-green batiks

(blocks, setting rectangles)

⅝ yard royal blue batik (binding)

3⅝ yards backing fabric

65×77" batting

Finished quilt: 59×70½"
Finished block: 6½×10"

Quantities are for 44/45"-wide, 100% cotton fabrics. **Measurements** include ¼" seam allowances. Sew with right sides together unless otherwise stated.

Size options: For a chart of optional sizes, turn to *Pattern Sheet 1.*

Designer Notes

Designer Amy Walsh likes how Asian graphics often repeat themselves and give a serene feeling. For this reason she is particularly fond of Japanese shoji screens, which she tried to emulate with this quilt.

"I selected the design of this quilt first, then looked for fabrics to fit the mood I wanted," Amy says. "I'm also a fan of quilts with alternate solid blocks because they go together quickly." Amy selected 20 different blue and blue-green batiks to make her quilt. Her fabric choices aid the illusion of three squares floating in the center of each pieced block. The melding of colors in the background prints is soft enough to hide the seam lines, fooling the eye.

Cut Fabrics

Cut pieces in the order that follows in each section.

From assorted blue and blue-green batiks, cut:
• 31—7×10½" setting rectangles
From royal blue batik, cut:
• 7—2½×42" binding strips

Cut and Assemble Blocks

These instructions result in one block. Repeat cutting and assembly instructions to make 32 blocks total.

continued

From one blue or blue-green batik, cut:
- 2—3×10½" rectangles
- 2—2×2½" rectangles
- 2—2×1¼" rectangles

From a second blue or blue-green batik, cut:
- 3—2" squares

1. Referring to **Diagram 1**, sew together blue or blue-green batik 2×2½" rectangles, 2" squares, and 2×1¼" rectangles to make a pieced row. Press seams in one direction. The pieced row should be 2×10½" including seam allowances.

2. Referring to **Diagram 2**, add blue or blue-green batik 3×10½" rectangles to long edges of pieced row to make a block. Press seams away from pieced row. The block should be 7×10½" including seam allowances.

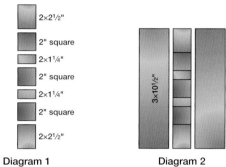

2×2½"

2" square

2×1¼"

2" square

2×1¼"

2" square

2×2½"

3×10½"

Diagram 1   Diagram 2

Zen

Assemble Quilt Top

Referring to **Quilt Assembly Diagram**, lay out blocks and assorted blue and blue-green batik setting rectangles in seven horizontal rows, alternating blocks and setting rectangles. Sew together pieces in each row. Press seams toward setting rectangles. Join rows to complete quilt top; press seams in one direction.

Finish Quilt

1. Layer quilt top, batting, and backing; baste. (For details, see Complete Quilt, *page 159*.)

2. Quilt as desired. Amy machine-quilted a meandering stitch that mimics rippling water (**Quilting Diagram**). "I love to use this design, especially on quilts that are made with Asian fabrics or were inspired by an Asian design," Amy says.

3. Bind with royal blue batik binding strips. (For details, see Complete Quilt.)

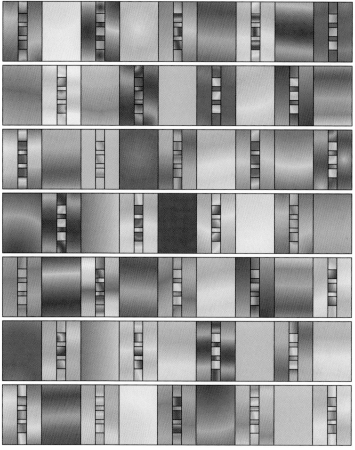

Quilt Assembly Diagram

Quilting Diagram

optional colors

Autumn Blaze

This version of *Zen* features shot cottons in a rainbow of hues. The warp and weft threads of these solids are different colors, giving the fabrics greater depth than you might expect. The simple design and artful arrangement of blocks provide an ideal opportunity for color experimentation.

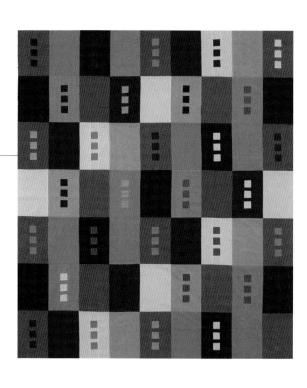

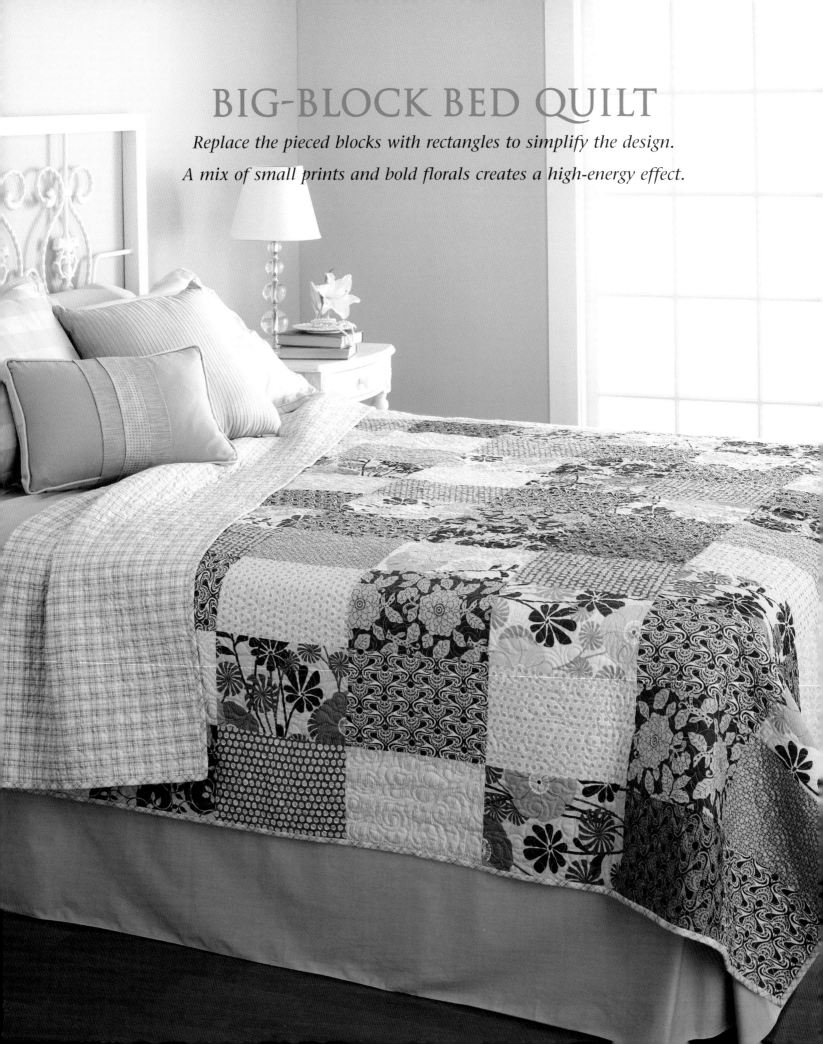

BIG-BLOCK BED QUILT

Replace the pieced blocks with rectangles to simplify the design.

A mix of small prints and bold florals creates a high-energy effect.

Materials

6½ yards total assorted prints and florals in pink, yellow, green, blue, and purple (rectangles)

⅞ yard green plaid (binding)

8¼ yards backing fabric

98×97" batting

Finished quilt: 91½×90½"

Cut Fabrics

Cut pieces in the following order.

From assorted prints and florals, cut:
• 126—7×10½" rectangles

From green plaid, cut:
• Enough 2½"-wide bias strips to total 380" for binding (For details, see Cut Bias Strips, *page 156*.)

Assemble Quilt Top

Referring to photo *below,* sew together assorted print and floral 7×10½" rectangles in nine horizontal rows. Press seams in one direction, alternating direction with each row. Join rows to complete quilt top. Press seams in one direction.

Finish Quilt

1. Layer quilt top, batting, and backing; baste. (For details, see Complete Quilt, *page 159.*) Quilt as desired.

2. Bind with green plaid bias binding strips. (For details, see Complete Quilt.)

REPRODUCTION PRINT THROW

Put a twist on a tradition—create an ultramodern design with reproduction fabrics.

Materials

2¼ yards total assorted medium and dark prints
   (blocks, setting rectangles)

1½ yards dark brown print (border, binding)

¼ yard total assorted light prints (blocks)

3⅓ yards backing fabric

60×65" batting

Finished quilt: 54×58½"

Cut Fabrics

Cut pieces in the order that follows in each section.

From assorted medium and dark prints, cut:
- 17—7×10½" setting rectangles

From dark brown print, cut:
- 6—4½×42" strips for border
- 6—2½×42" binding strips

Cut and Assemble Blocks

These instructions result in one block. Repeat cutting and assembly steps to make 18 blocks total.

From one medium or dark print, cut:
- 2—3×10½" rectangles
- 2—2×2½" rectangles
- 2—2×1¼" rectangles

From one light print, cut:
- 3—2" squares

Referring to Cut and Assemble Blocks, *page 62,* steps 1 and 2, use medium or dark print rectangles and light print 2" squares to make a block.

Assemble Quilt Center

1. Referring to photo, *right,* lay out blocks and setting rectangles in five horizontal rows, alternating blocks and setting rectangles. Sew together pieces in each row. Press seams toward setting rectangles.

2. Join rows to make quilt center. Press seams in one direction. The quilt center should be 46×50½" including seam allowances.

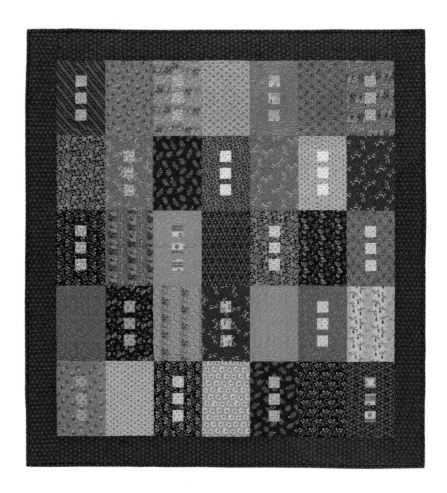

Add Border

1. Cut and piece dark brown print 4½x42" strips to make:
- 2—4½×58½" border strips
- 2—4½×46" border strips

2. Sew short border strips to short edges of quilt center. Add long border strips to remaining edges to complete quilt top. Press all seams toward border.

Finish Quilt

1. Layer quilt top, batting, and backing; baste. (For details, see Complete Quilt, *page 159.*)

2. Quilt as desired. Allover swirl designs are machine-stitched across this quilt top.

3. Bind with dark brown print binding strips. (For details, see Complete Quilt.)

TINY
TREASURES

Intricate piecing and attention to detail are the
hallmarks of these small, scrappy projects. Make
hearts melt with the gift of a petite table topper,
pretty wall hanging, or more. Best of all, satisfy your
urge to try out a new block or two without the time
commitment of a larger quilt.

86

85

88

76

ROLLING *Stones*

This miniature quilt from designer Ann Hermes showcases authentic 1880s fabrics in traditional Pennsylvania German colors of chrome yellow, double pink, and overdyed green.

Materials

9×22" piece (fat eighth) yellow print (blocks)

9×22" piece (fat eighth) pink print (blocks)

¼ yard total assorted green prints (blocks, sashing, border)

9×22" piece (fat eighth) gold print (sashing)

9×22" piece (fat eighth) black print (binding)

18×22" piece (fat quarter) backing fabric

18" square batting

Finished quilt: 14" square
Finished block: 4½" square

Quantities are for 44/45"-wide, 100% cotton fabrics. **Measurements** include ¼" seam allowances. Sew with right sides together unless otherwise stated.

Designer Notes

Designer Ann Hermes specializes in making miniature quilts with her collection of antique fabrics. Calicos in this project date to circa 1880 and re-create a vivid color combination common in southeastern Pennsylvania quilts.

Foundation-Piecing Alternative

For precise blocks in doll quilts or miniature quilts, some quilters prefer paper piecing instead of traditional piecing. See *Pattern Sheet 2* for Square-in-a-Square and Flying Geese foundation patterns.

Cut Fabrics

Cut pieces in the following order.

From yellow print, cut:
- 16—1¼×2" rectangles
- 32—1⅝" squares, cutting each in half diagonally for 64 triangles total

From pink print, cut:
- 16—1¼×2" rectangles
- 17—1½" squares

From one green print, cut:
- 2—2×14" border strips
- 2—2×11" border strips

From remaining assorted green prints, cut:
- 4—2" squares
- 2—1⅝" squares, cutting each in half diagonally for 4 triangles total
- 48—1¼" squares (24 pairs of matching squares)

From gold print, cut:
- 24—1¼×2" rectangles

From black print, cut:
- 3—1¼×22" binding strips

continued

Assemble Square-in-a-Square Units

1. Sew yellow print triangles to opposite edges of a pink print 1½" square (**Diagram 1**). Press seams toward triangles. Sew yellow print triangles to remaining edges to make a yellow Square-in-a-Square unit. Press seams toward triangles. The unit should be 2" square including seam allowances.

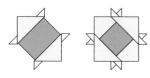

Diagram 1

2. Repeat Step 1 to make 16 yellow Square-in-a-Square units total.

3. Using green print triangles and a pink print 1½" square, repeat Step 1 to make a green Square-in-a-Square unit.

Assemble Blocks

1. Sew together a yellow print 1¼×2" rectangle and a pink print 1¼×2" rectangle to make a rectangle-square unit (**Diagram 2**). Press seam in one direction. The unit should be 2" square including seam allowances. Repeat to make 16 rectangle-square units total.

Diagram 2

2. Referring to **Diagram 3**, sew together four rectangle-square units, four yellow Square-in-a-Square units, and one green print 2" square in rows. Press seams toward rectangle-square units. Join rows to make a Rolling Stones block. Press seams toward middle row. The block should be 5" square including seam allowances. Repeat to make four Rolling Stones blocks total.

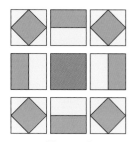

Diagram 3

Assemble Flying Geese Units

1. Use a pencil to mark a diagonal line on wrong side of each assorted green print 1¼" square.

2. Align a marked green print 1¼" square with one end of a gold print 1¼×2" rectangle (**Diagram 4**; note direction of drawn line). Sew on drawn line; trim excess, leaving a ¼" seam allowance. Press open attached triangle.

Diagram 4

3. Align and sew a second marked green print 1¼" square to opposite end of gold print rectangle (**Diagram 4**). Trim and press as before to make a Flying Geese unit. The unit should be 1¼×2" including seam allowances.

4. Repeat steps 2 and 3 to make 24 Flying Geese units total.

Assemble Quilt Top

1. Referring to **Quilt Assembly Diagram**, join six Flying Geese units to make a sashing strip. Press seams in one direction. The sashing strip should be 2×5" including seam allowances. Repeat to make four sashing strips total.

2. Referring to **Quilt Assembly Diagram**, lay out Rolling Stones blocks, sashing strips, and the green Square-in-a-Square unit in rows.

3. Sew together pieces in each row. Press seams toward blocks and green Square-in-a-Square unit.

4. Join rows to make quilt center. Press seams toward top and bottom rows. The quilt center should be 11" square including seam allowances.

5. Sew short green print border strips to opposite edges of quilt center. Add long green print border strips to remaining edges to complete quilt top. Press all seams toward border.

Rolling Stones

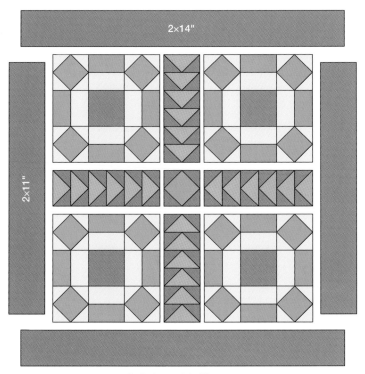

Quilt Assembly Diagram

Finish Quilt

1. Layer quilt top, batting, and backing; baste. (For details, see Complete Quilt, *page 159.*)

2. Quilt as desired. In each block, Ann hand-quilted an X and a cross, continuing the design into the sashing strips and border **(Quilting Diagram).**

3. Bind with black print binding strips using a single-fold method. (Without folding binding strip in half lengthwise, follow instructions in Complete Quilt. Fold raw edge under ¼" before hand-stitching binding to quilt backing.)

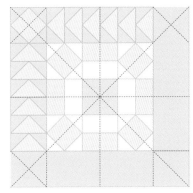

Quilting Diagram

optional colors

Silken Stones

Quilt tester Laura Boehnke selected 100% silks in onyx, sapphire, burgundy, and gold to make her version of *Rolling Stones.*

"The solid fabric gives the quilt an Amish feel," Laura says. "But at the same time, it's very contemporary and modern." If you have trouble sewing with silks or silky fabrics, consider fusing a very lightweight interfacing to the wrong side of the fabric before cutting.

TOKEN QUILTS

Experiment with color placement or unit arrangement to create an altogether different look in a single block. Give the tiny quilt to a friend as a token of your affection.

Materials for Token Quilt No. 1

12" square gold tone-on-tone

6" square navy blue print

6" square green tone-on-tone

3×28" rectangle red print

7" square backing fabric

7" square batting

Finished quilt: 5" square

Cut Fabrics

Cut pieces in the following order.

From gold tone-on-tone, cut:
- 4—1¼×2" rectangles
- 8—1⅝" squares, cutting each in half diagonally for 16 triangles total

From navy blue print, cut:
- 4—1½" squares

From green tone-on-tone, cut:
- 4—1¼×2" rectangles

From red print, cut:
- 1—1¼×22" binding strip
- 1—2" square

Assemble Quilt Top

1. Referring to Assemble Square-in-a-Square Units, Step 1, *page 74*, use gold tone-on-tone triangles and navy print 1½" squares to make four Square-in-a-Square units.

2. Referring to Assemble Blocks, Step 1, *page 74*, use gold tone-on-tone and green tone-on-tone 1¼×2" rectangles to make four rectangle-square units.

3. Referring to **Token Quilt No. 1 Assembly Diagram**,

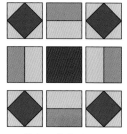

Token Quilt No. 1
Assembly Diagram

lay out Square-in-a-Square units, rectangle-square units, and red print 2" square in three rows. Sew together pieces in each row. Press seams toward rectangle-square units. Join rows to make quilt top. Press seams toward center row.

Finish Quilt

1. Layer quilt top, batting, and backing; baste. (For details, see Complete Quilt, *page 159.*)

2. Quilt as desired. This quilt was machine-quilted in the ditch between units in horizontal and vertical rows.

3. Referring to Finish Quilt, Step 3, *page 75*, bind with red print binding strips using a single-fold method.

Materials for Token Quilt No. 2

12" square tan print

8" square navy blue print

4×26" rectangle green tone-on-tone

7" square backing fabric

7" square batting

Finished quilt: 5" square

Cut Fabrics

Cut pieces in the following order.

From tan print, cut:
- 8—1¼×2" rectangles
- 8—1⅝" squares, cutting each in half diagonally for 16 triangles total
- 1—1½" square

From navy blue print, cut:
- 2—1⅝" squares, cutting each in half diagonally for 4 triangles total
- 4—1½" squares

From green tone-on-tone, cut:
- 1—1¼×22" binding strip
- 16—1¼" squares

Assemble Quilt Top

1. Referring to Assemble Square-in-a-Square Units, Step 1, *page 74,* use tan print triangles and navy blue print 1½" squares to make four navy blue Square-in-a-Square units. Then use navy blue print triangles and tan print 1½" square to make one tan Square-in-a-Square unit.

2. Referring to Assemble Flying Geese Units, steps 1–3, *page 74,* use tan print 1¼×2" rectangles and green tone-on-tone 1¼" squares to make eight Flying Geese units.

3. Lay out Flying Geese units and Square-in-a-Square units in three rows (**Token Quilt**

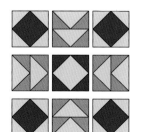

Token Quilt No. 2
Assembly Diagram

No. 2 Assembly Diagram). Sew together Flying Geese units in pairs; then join pairs to Square-in-a-Square units in each row, pressing seams toward Flying Geese units. Join rows to make quilt top. Press seams toward middle row.

Finish Quilt

1. Layer quilt top, batting, and backing; baste. (For details, see Complete Quilt, *page 159.*)

2. Quilt as desired. This quilt was machine-quilted in the ditch around the navy blue Square-in-a-Square units and around the tan print square in the center unit.

3. Referring to Finish Quilt, Step 3, *page 75,* bind with green tone-on-tone binding strips using a single-fold method.

SIGNATURE WALL HANGING

Collect autographs on solid fabric and center them in each Rolling Stones block.

Materials

12" square solid beige (blocks)

⅓ yard red-and-tan stripe (blocks)

⅓ yard blue-and-tan stripe (blocks)

½ yard total assorted red prints (blocks, sashing)

½ yard total assorted navy blue prints (blocks, sashing)

½ yard tan print (sashing)

⅝ yard mottled red (sashing, border, binding)

1 yard backing fabric

32" square batting

Freezer paper

Fine-point permanent marking pen

Finished quilt: 26" square
Finished block: 4½" square

Rolling Stones

Foundation-Piecing Alternative

For an alternative piecing method, see Foundation-Piecing Alternative, *page 73.*

Cut Fabrics

Cut pieces in the order that follows. Cut red-and-tan stripe and blue-and-tan stripe rectangles with stripes perpendicular to long edges. To get same effect as on the featured quilt's Square-in-a-Square units (**Diagram 5,** *page 80*), cut red-and-tan stripe and blue-and-tan stripe squares on the bias. Then cut in half diagonally so stripes run perpendicular to the cut edge.

From solid beige, cut:
- 16—2" squares

From red-and-tan stripe, cut:
- 32—1¼×2" rectangles
- 64—1⅝" squares, cutting each in half diagonally for 128 triangles total

From blue-and-tan stripe, cut:
- 32—1¼×2" rectangles
- 64—1⅝" squares, cutting each in half diagonally for 128 triangles total

From assorted red prints, cut:
- 104—1¼×2" rectangles (8 sets of 4 matching rectangles and 72 assorted red print rectangles)
- 28—1½" squares (7 sets of 4 matching squares)

From assorted navy blue prints, cut:
- 104—1¼×2" rectangles (8 sets of 4 matching rectangles and 72 assorted navy print rectangles)
- 36—1½" squares (9 sets of 4 matching squares)

From tan print, cut:
- 8—1⅝" squares, cutting each in half diagonally for 16 triangles total
- 5—1½" squares
- 288—1¼" squares

From mottled red, cut:
- 3—2½×42" binding strips
- 2—2×26" border strips
- 2—2×23" border strips
- 10—1⅝" squares, cutting each in half diagonally for 20 triangles total
- 4—1½" squares

From freezer paper, cut:
- 16—1½" squares

continued

Prepare Autographed Block Centers

To stabilize the fabric and create guidelines for writing, use a hot, dry iron to press a freezer paper 1½" square centered on the back of each solid beige 2" square. (You may wish to create extra fabric squares backed with freezer paper to allow people to practice writing.) Collect signatures on fabric squares, advising those writing to use a light touch, write slowly, and avoid writing in the seam allowances.

Assemble Square-in-a-Square Units

1. Referring to Assemble Square-in-a-Square Units, Step 1, *page 74*, and **Diagram 5**, use four matching navy blue print 1½" squares and 16 red-and-tan stripe or blue-and-tan stripe triangles to make four matching navy blue Square-in-a-Square units. Repeat to make nine sets total of four navy blue Square-in-a-Square units.

2. Repeat Step 1 using a set of four red print 1½" squares to make four matching red Square-in-a-Square units (**Diagram 6**). Repeat to make seven sets total of four red Square-in-a-Square units.

Diagram 5   Diagram 6

3. Using mottled red triangles and tan print 1½" squares, repeat Step 1 to make five tan Square-in-a-Square units (**Diagram 7**). Then use tan print triangles and mottled red 1½" squares to make four mottled red Square-in-a-Square units (**Diagram 8**).

Diagram 7   Diagram 8

Assemble Blocks

1. Referring to Assemble Blocks, Step 1, *page 74,* use four matching red print 1¼×2" rectangles and four red-and-tan stripe or blue-and-tan stripe triangles 1¼×2" rectangles to make four matching red rectangle-square units. Repeat to make eight sets total of four red rectangle-square units.

2. Repeat Step 1 using a set of four navy blue print 1¼×2" rectangles to make four matching navy blue rectangle-square units. Repeat to make eight

sets total of four matching navy blue rectangle-square units.

3. Gather a set of four matching navy blue Square-in-a-Square units, a set of four matching red rectangle-square units, and one solid beige 2" square. Referring to Assemble Blocks, Step 2, *page 74*, and **Diagram 9**, use pieces to make a Rolling Stones A block. Repeat to make eight Rolling Stones A blocks total.

4. Repeat Step 3 using a set of four matching red Square-in-a-Square units, a set of four matching navy blue rectangle-square units, and one solid beige 2" square to make a Rolling Stones B block (**Diagram 10**). Repeat to make seven Rolling Stones B blocks total.

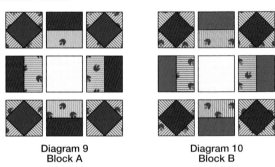

Diagram 9   Diagram 10
Block A   Block B

5. Repeat Step 3 using remaining set of four matching navy blue Square-in-a-Square units, remaining set of four matching navy blue rectangle-square units, and remaining solid beige 2" square to make a Rolling Stones C block (**Diagram 11**).

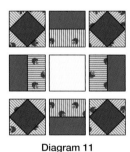

Diagram 11
Block C

Assemble Flying Geese Units

1. Referring to Assemble Flying Geese Units, steps 1–3, *page 74*, use tan print 1¼" squares and assorted navy blue print 1¼×2" rectangles to make 72 navy blue Flying Geese units total.

2. Repeat Step 1 using tan print 1¼" squares and assorted red print 1¼×2" rectangles to make 72 red Flying Geese units total.

Assemble Quilt Top

Instructions that follow specify alternating placement of red and navy blue Flying Geese units in the sashing strips. To add interest, the designer of this quilt sometimes varied from that placement.

1. Referring to **Quilt Assembly Diagram**, and Assemble Quilt Top, Step 1, *page 74,* join three navy blue and three red Flying Geese units, alternating units, to make a sashing strip. Repeat to make 24 sashing strips total, 12 with a navy blue unit at beginning of strip and 12 with a red unit.

2. Referring to **Quilt Assembly Diagram**, lay out blocks, sashing strips, and the five tan and four mottled red Square-in-a-Square units in seven horizontal rows.

3. Sew together pieces in each row. Press seams away from sashing strips. Join rows to make quilt center. Press seams toward block rows. The quilt center should be 23" square including seam allowances.

4. Sew short mottled red border strips to opposite edges of quilt center. Add long mottled red border strips to remaining edges to complete quilt top. Press all seams toward border.

Finish Quilt

1. Layer quilt top, batting, and backing; baste. (For details, see Complete Quilt, *page 159.*) Quilt as desired.

2. Bind with mottled red binding strips. (For details, see Complete Quilt.)

Quilt Assembly Diagram

STAR
Vine

Deck out a table during the holidays with this festive quilt from designer Renée Plains, featuring fusible-appliquéd starflowers on blue ticking backgrounds.

Materials

⅜ yard green print (vine and leaf appliqués, sashing squares)

⅝ yard red print (starflower appliqués, sashing, binding)

8" square gold print (starflower center appliqués)

¼ yard blue ticking (appliqué foundations)

⅛ yard cream print (sashing)

⅞ yard backing fabric

30" square batting

1 yard lightweight fusible web

Embroidery floss: red, green, gold

Finished quilt: 23¼" square
Finished block: 8" square

Quantities are for 44/45"-wide, 100% cotton fabrics.
Measurements include ¼" seam allowances. Sew with right sides together unless otherwise stated.

Cut Fabrics

Cut pieces in the following order. Patterns are on *Pattern Sheet 2*. To use fusible web for appliquéing, complete the following steps.

1. Lay fusible web, paper side up, over patterns. Use a pencil to trace each pattern the number of times indicated in cutting instructions, leaving ½" between tracings. Cut out each fusible-web shape roughly ¼" outside traced lines.

2. Following the manufacturer's instructions, press each fusible-web shape onto wrong side of designated fabric; let cool. Cut out fabric shapes on drawn lines. Peel off paper backings.

From green print, cut:
• 9—2¾" sashing squares
• 4 *each* of patterns B, C, and D
• 40 of Pattern E
From red print, cut:
• 3—2½×42" binding strips
• 6—1¼×42" strips
• 21 of Pattern A
From gold print, cut:
• 21 of Pattern F
From blue ticking, cut:
• 4—8½" foundation squares
From cream print, cut:
• 3—1¼×42" strips

continued

To blanket-stitch, pull your needle up at A (**Blanket Stitch Diagram**), form a reverse L shape with floss, and hold the angle of L shape in place with your thumb. Push needle down at B and come up at C to secure stitch. Continue in same manner around entire shape.

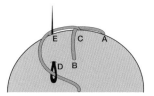

Blanket Stitch Diagram

3. Repeat steps 1 and 2 to make four appliquéd blocks total. In two blocks, blue ticking stripe should be horizontal; in two remaining blocks, it should be vertical.

4. Referring to photo, *left,* position a red print starflower and gold print starflower center on a green print sashing square. Fuse and blanket-stitch in place to make an appliquéd sashing square. Repeat to make nine appliquéd sashing squares total.

Assemble Quilt Top

1. Aligning long edges, sew a red print 1¼×42" strip to each long edge of a cream print 1¼×42" strip to make a strip set. Press seams toward red print strips. Repeat to make three strip sets total. Cut strip sets into 12—2¾×8½" sashing strips total.

2. Referring to photo, *left,* lay out appliquéd blocks, sashing strips, and appliquéd sashing squares in five rows, rotating blocks as shown.

3. Sew together pieces in each row. Press seams toward sashing strips. Join rows to make quilt top. Press seams toward sashing rows.

Finish Quilt

1. Layer quilt top, batting, and backing; baste. (For details, see Complete Quilt, *page 159.*) Quilt as desired.

2. Bind with red print binding strips. (For details, see Complete Quilt.)

Appliqué Blocks and Sashing Squares

1. Referring to **Appliqué Placement Diagram**, position green print stems and leaves, red print starflowers, and gold print starflower centers on a blue ticking 8½" foundation square, overlapping as shown; fuse in place.

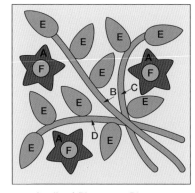

Appliqué Placement Diagram

2. Using two strands of matching embroidery floss, hand-blanket-stitch around each appliqué shape to make an appliquéd block.

EMBELLISHED TEA TOWELS

Jazz up handmade or store-bought kitchen linens with starflower appliqués.

Materials for two towels

Scraps of assorted bright prints (appliqués)

1½ yards green plaid homespun *or* two purchased tea towels

Machine-embroidery thread: light green

Lightweight fusible web

Finished towel: 20½×28½"

Cut Fabrics

This project uses *Star Vine* patterns A and F on *Pattern Sheet 2*. To use fusible web for appliquéing, refer to Cut Fabrics, steps 1 and 2, *page 83*. If you are using purchased tea towels, skip Cut and Hem Tea Towels instructions below.

From assorted bright prints, cut:
• 12 *each* of patterns A and F

Cut and Hem Tea Towels

From green plaid homespun, cut:
• 2—22×30" rectangles

Fold under one long edge of a green plaid 22×30" rectangle ⅜"; press. Fold over ⅜" again; press. Backstitching at beginning and end of seam, topstitch close to first folded edge to hem. Repeat with remaining long edge. In the same manner, hem short edges of green plaid rectangle to make a tea towel; press. The tea towel should be 20½×28½". Repeat to make a second tea towel.

Appliqué Tea Towels

Referring to photo, *below,* lay out five each of patterns A and F on one end of towel; fuse in place. Fuse one each of patterns A and F on opposite end of towel. Using light green thread, machine-blanket-stitch around each appliqué shape to complete towel. Repeat to appliqué second tea towel.

FELTED WOOL TOTE

An appliqué bouquet cut from scraps of hand-dyed, felted wool gives an inexpensive tote a custom look.

Materials

8½" square mottled brown felted wool (appliqué foundation)

3×12" piece green felted wool (stem appliqués)

Scraps of assorted felted wool in red, purple, light blue, and yellow (appliqués)

Perle cotton No. 5: red, purple, light blue, yellow

Embroidery floss: brown

Freezer paper

Black tote bag (at least 15" in height and width)

Cut Fabrics

Cut pieces in the order that follows. This project uses *Star Vine* patterns on *Pattern Sheet 2*.

To felt wool, machine-wash it in a hot-water-wash, cool-rinse cycle with a small amount of detergent; machine-dry on high heat and steam-press.

To use freezer paper for cutting appliqué shapes, complete the following steps.

1. Lay freezer paper, shiny side down, over patterns. Use a pencil to trace each pattern the number of times indicated in cutting instructions, leaving ¼" between tracings. Cut out freezer-paper shapes roughly ⅛" outside drawn lines.

2. Using a hot, dry iron, press each freezer-paper shape, shiny side down, onto right side of designated wool; let cool. Cut out wool shapes on drawn lines. Peel off freezer paper.

From green wool, cut:
• 1 *each* of patterns B, C, and D
From red wool, cut:
• 3 of Pattern A
From purple wool, cut:
• 7 of Pattern E
From light blue wool, cut:
• 3 of Pattern E
From yellow wool, cut:
• 3 of Pattern F

Appliqué Tote Bag

1. Referring to photo, *right,* and Appliqué Blocks and Sashing Squares, Step 1, *page 84,* baste appliqué shapes on brown wool 8½" foundation square. (Block will be mirror-image of **Appliqué Placement Diagram**.)

2. Use matching perle cotton to whipstitch around each appliqué shape to make an appliquéd block.

3. Referring to photo, center appliquéd block on tote bag; pin or baste in place. Using six strands of brown embroidery floss, whipstitch around edges to secure block and complete tote bag.

VINTAGE
Voyage

Show off even the smallest scraps of reproduction or vintage fabrics in this petite quilt from designer Ann Hermes. Bolder pieces set sail in the large triangles, while shirtings and small prints balance out the look.

Materials

⅓ yard total assorted light prints in tan, blue, and
    ecru (large and small triangle-squares)

⅓ yard total assorted dark prints in navy blue,
    brown, and red (large and small triangle-squares)

Scraps of solid Cheddar yellow and pink print
    (small triangle-squares)

6" square rust pin dot (setting squares)

18×22" piece (fat quarter) brown floral (border)

¼ yard dark brown print (binding)

⅝ yard backing fabric

20" square batting

Finished quilt: 15½" square

Quantities are for 44/45"-wide, 100% cotton fabrics.
Measurements include ¼" seam allowances. Sew
with right sides together unless otherwise stated.

Cut Fabrics

Cut pieces in the following order.

From assorted light prints, cut:
- 5—3⅞" squares
- 48—1¾" squares

From navy blue print, cut:
- 1—3⅞" square

From brown print, cut:
- 2—3⅞" squares

From red print, cut:
- 2—3⅞" squares

From remaining dark print scraps, cut:
- 41—1¾" squares

From solid Cheddar yellow, cut:
- 4—1¾" squares

From pink print, cut:
- 3—1¾" squares

From rust pin dot, cut:
- 4—2" setting squares

From brown floral, cut:
- 2—2×15½" border strips
- 2—2×12½" border strips

From dark brown print, cut:
- 2—2½×42" binding strips

continued

Assemble Triangle-Squares

1. Use a pencil to mark a diagonal line on wrong side of each light print 3⅞" and 1¼" square.

2. Layer a marked 3⅞" square atop a navy blue print 3⅞" square. Sew together with two seams, stitching ¼" on each side of drawn line **(Diagram 1)**.

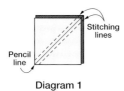

Diagram 1   Diagram 2   Diagram 3

3. Cut apart on drawn line to make two triangle units **(Diagram 2)**. Press each triangle unit open, pressing seams toward navy blue print triangles, to make two large triangle-squares **(Diagram 3)**. Each triangle-square should be 3½" square including seam allowances.

4. Repeat steps 2 and 3 with remaining marked light print and dark print 3⅞" squares to make 10 large triangle-squares total (you will use nine).

5. Repeat steps 2 and 3 with marked light print 1¾" squares and the dark print, solid Cheddar yellow, and pink print 1¾" squares to make 96 small triangle-squares total. Trim each small triangle-square to 1¼" square including seam allowances.

Assemble Quilt Top

1. Referring to **Quilt Assembly Diagram**, lay out large and small triangle-squares and setting squares. For added interest, designer Ann Hermes turned one small triangle-square 180° from the rest.

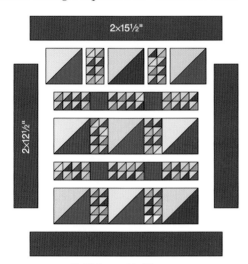

Quilt Assembly Diagram

2. Sew together small triangle-squares in strips of four. In each pair of strips, press seams in opposite directions. Join strips in pairs to make pieced sashing rectangles; press seams in one direction. Each rectangle should be 2×3½" including seam allowances.

3. Sew together large triangle-squares, pieced sashing rectangles, and setting squares in five rows. Press seams away from pieced sashing rectangles.

Join rows to make quilt center. Press seams in one direction. The quilt center should be 12½" square including seam allowances.

4. Sew short brown floral border strips to opposite edges of quilt center. Add long brown floral border strips to remaining edges to complete quilt top. Press all seams toward border.

Finish Quilt

1. Layer quilt top, batting and backing; baste. (For details, see Complete Quilt, *page 159.*)

2. Quilt as desired. Ann stitched in the ditch between rows, then stitched diagonally in one direction across the quilt top (**Quilting Diagram**).

3. Bind with dark brown print binding strips. (For details, see Complete Quilt.)

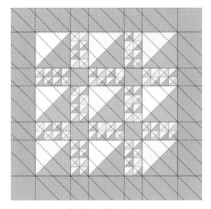

Quilting Diagram

optional colors

The Colors of Spring

By making small triangle-squares from tone-on-tone rose prints, quilt tester Laura Boehnke created pieced sashing rectangles that flow together almost like a watercolor painting. The large triangle-squares feature red and yellow florals with a larger scale.

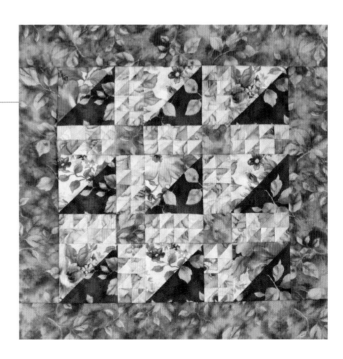

KID-FRIENDLY PILLOW

Fussy-cut novelty prints to make a bold statement on a colorful pillow.

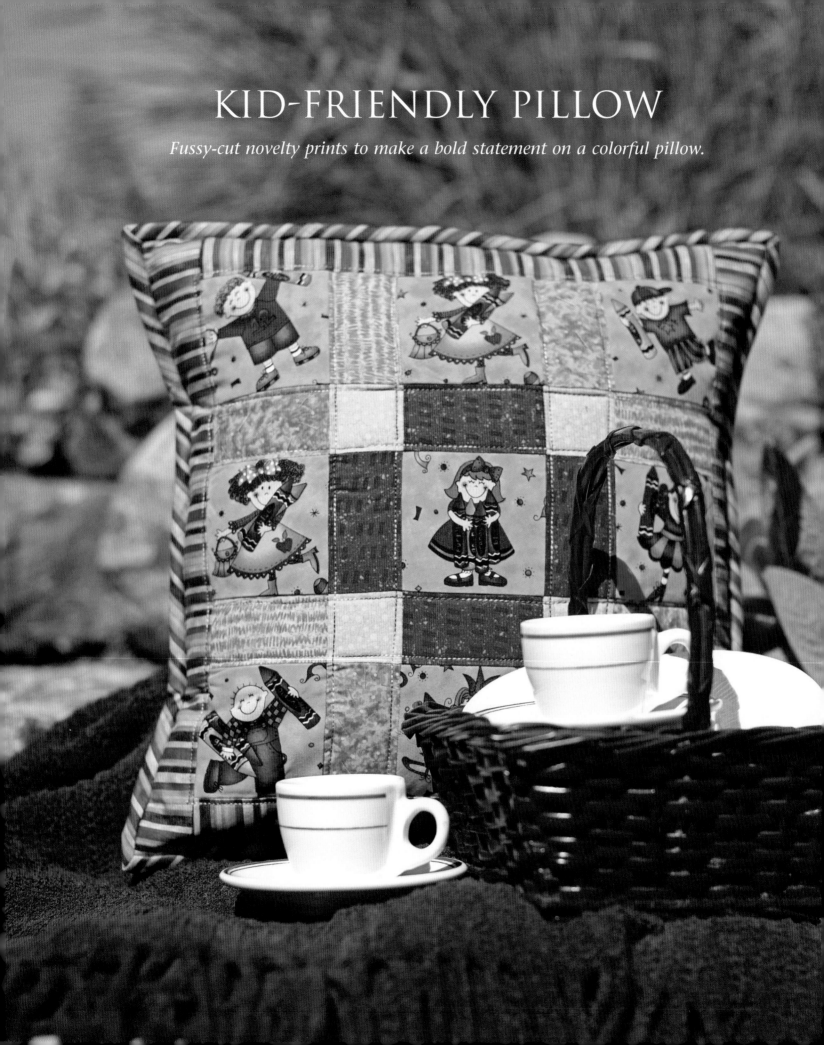

Materials

¼ yard novelty print (pillow center)

10" square *each* of green, blue, and red tone-on-tones (pillow center)

Scrap of yellow tone-on-tone (pillow center)

1¼ yards multicolor stripe (border, pillow back, binding)

20" square muslin (lining)

20" square batting

15"-square pillow form

Finished pillow: 15½" square

Cut Fabrics

Cut pieces in the following order.

From novelty print, fussy-cut:
• 9—3½" squares
From *each* of green, blue, and red tone-on-tone, cut:
• 4—2×3½" rectangles
From yellow tone-on-tone, cut:
• 4—2" squares
From multicolor stripe, cut:
• 2—15½×19½" rectangles
• 1—18" square, cutting it into enough 2½"-wide bias strips to total 75" for binding (For details, see Cut Bias Strips, *page 156.*)
• 2—2×15½" border strips
• 2—2×12½" border strips

Assemble Pillow Top

1. Referring to **Pillow Assembly Diagram**, lay out novelty print 3½" squares; green, blue, and red tone-on-tone 2×3½" rectangles; and yellow tone-on-tone 2" squares in five rows.

2. Sew together pieces in each row. Press seams toward tone-on-tone rectangles. Join rows to make pillow center. Press seams in one direction. The pillow center should be 12½" square including seam allowances.

3. Sew multicolor stripe 2×12½" border strips to opposite edges of pillow center. Join multicolor

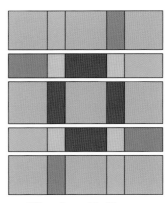

Pillow Assembly Diagram

stripe 2×15½" border strips to remaining edges to complete pillow top. Press all seams toward border.

Finish Pillow

1. Layer pillow top, batting, and muslin lining; baste. (For details, see Complete Quilt, *page 159.*)

2. Quilt as desired. Using variegated thread, the featured pillow top is outline-quilted inside each tone-on-tone piece and around the border.

3. With wrong side inside, fold each multicolor stripe 15½×19½" rectangle in half to make two 9¾×15½" double-thick pillow back rectangles. Referring to **Diagram 4**, overlap folded edges by about 4" to make a 15½"-square pillow back. Baste along top and bottom edges to secure pieces.

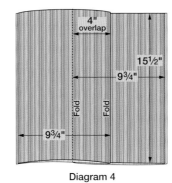

Diagram 4

4. With wrong sides together, layer pillow top and pillow back; pin or baste edges. Sew together through all layers to make pillow cover.

5. Bind with multicolor stripe bias binding strips. (For details, see Complete Quilt.) Insert pillow form through opening in pillow back.

Vintage Voyage

CUSTOM
JOURNAL
COVER

For a quick gift, clothe a standard journal
with a jacket pieced from triangle-squares.

Materials

- 2—9×22" pieces (fat eighths) assorted light green solids (journal cover)
- 2—9×22" pieces (fat eighths) assorted aqua solids (journal cover)
- 8" square solid blue (journal cover)
- 12" square solid rust (journal cover)
- ½ yard solid dark blue (journal cover)
- ½ yard flannel (lining)
- 7½×9¾" composition book

Finished journal cover: 7½×10" (fits a standard-size composition book)

Cut Fabrics

Cut pieces in the following order.

From solid light green No. 1, cut:
- 1—3⅞" square
- 6—1¾" squares

From solid light green No. 2, cut:
- 6—1¾" squares

From solid aqua No. 1, cut:
- 1—3⅞" square
- 5—1¾" squares

From solid aqua No. 2, cut:
- 4—2" setting squares
- 3—1¾" squares

From solid blue, cut:
- 8—1¾" squares

From solid rust, cut:
- 2—4¼×6½" rectangles
- 1—1¾" square

From solid dark blue, cut:
- 1—14×15¾" rectangle
- 1—8¼×14" rectangle
- 4—1¾" squares

From flannel, cut:
- 1—14×29½" rectangle

Assemble Journal Cover Center

1. Use a pencil to mark a diagonal line on wrong side of solid light green No. 1—3⅞" square. Also mark a diagonal line on wrong side of each solid light green No. 2—1¾" square, four solid light green No. 1—1¾" squares, four solid aqua No. 1—1¾" squares, and two solid blue 1¾" squares.

2. Referring to Assemble Triangle-Squares, steps 2 and 3, *page 90,* use marked solid light green No. 1—3⅞" square and solid aqua No. 1—3⅞" square to make two large triangle-squares (you'll use one large triangle-square).

3. Referring to Assemble Triangle-Squares, Step 5, used marked solid 1¾" squares and unmarked solid 1¾" squares to make 32 small triangle-squares total.

4. Referring to **Diagram 5,** lay out one large triangle-square, 32 small triangle-squares, and solid aqua No. 2 setting squares in three rows.

5. Referring to Assemble Quilt Top, Step 2, *page 91,* sew together small triangle-squares in strips to make four pieced sashing rectangles.

6. Sew together pieces in each row **(Diagram 5).** Press seams away from pieced sashing rectangles. Join rows to make journal cover center. Press seams toward middle row. The journal cover center should be 6½" square including seam allowances.

Finish Journal Cover

1. Referring to **Diagram 6,** join solid rust 4¼×6½" rectangles to top and bottom edges of journal cover center. Press seams toward solid rust.

2. Sew solid dark blue 14×15¾" rectangle to left-hand edge of journal cover center **(Diagram 6).** Add solid dark blue 8¼×14" rectangle to right-hand edge of journal cover center to complete journal cover top. Press seams toward solid dark blue rectangles. The journal cover top should be 29½×14" including seam allowances.

3. Layer journal cover top and flannel 14×29½" rectangle wrong sides together. Zigzag-stitch around all edges of rectangles. Quilt as desired. The featured journal cover top is quilted in the ditch in some seams of the journal cover center, and parallel vertical lines are stitched ¾" apart in the solid dark blue rectangles.

4. Referring to **Diagram 7,** turn under short edges of layered rectangles ¾"; topstitch close to edges. Then fold each short edge 6½" toward center to make a 15×14" rectangle. Sew 2" from each long edge **(Diagram 7).**

5. To reduce bulk, trim away upper layer of journal cover seam allowances. Trim bottom layer seam allowances at an angle **(Diagram 8).** Turn cover right side out and insert composition book.

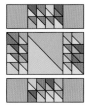

Diagram 5

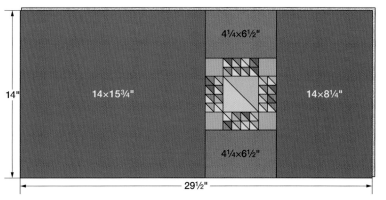

Diagram 6

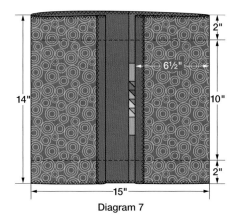

Diagram 7

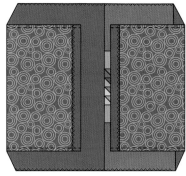

Diagram 8

ROTARY-CUT
CREATIONS

*Slice and dice your way to a stunning new quilt in
no time with these patterns designed for your rotary
cutter. Whip out your self-healing mat and acrylic
ruler, and roll on—no scissors necessary!*

*Remember: Measure twice, cut once. Before you
know it, you'll have accurate pieces ready to sew into
something wonderful.*

116

112

103

GIVE THANKS

122

SQUARE
Deal

Designers Barbara Groves and Mary Jacobson gave square blocks a dynamic twist by experimenting with advancing and receding hues.

Materials

6¼ yards total assorted prints in red, orange, yellow,

   green, blue, purple, and pink (blocks, binding)

½ yard *each* of pink, yellow, blue, and green prints

   (border)

4¼ yards solid white (blocks)

8½ yards backing fabric

102" square batting

Finished quilt: 96" square
Finished blocks: 12½" square

Quantities are for 44/45"-wide, 100% cotton fabrics.
Measurements include ¼" seam allowances. Sew with right sides together unless otherwise stated.

Size options: For a chart of optional sizes, turn to *Pattern Sheet 1.*

Designer Notes

Designers Barbara Groves and Mary Jacobson of Me and My Sister Designs added a playful sense of movement to this quilt by alternating the placement of the white and print pieces in the two blocks. "The difference between the blocks makes the rows appear to be wiggling back and forth through the quilt center," Mary says. They also included some surprises in their color choices. "We sprinkled in a few red prints to add pop to the mostly pastel-and-white quilt top," Barbara says.

Cut Fabrics

Cut pieces in the order that follows in each section.

From assorted prints, cut:
* Enough 2½"-wide strips in lengths varying from 12" to 40" to total 400" in length for binding

From *each* of the pink, yellow, blue, and green prints, cut:
* 3—4½×42" strips for border

Cut and Assemble Block A

The following instructions result in one block A. Repeat cutting and assembly steps to make 25 A blocks total.

From one assorted print, cut:
* 1—3" square

From a second assorted print, cut:
* 2—2×8" rectangles
* 2—2×5" rectangles

From a third assorted print, cut:
* 2—2×13" rectangles
* 2—2×10" rectangles

From solid white, cut:
* 2—1½×10" rectangles
* 2—1½×8" rectangles
* 2—1½×5" rectangles
* 2—1½×3" rectangles

continued

1. Referring to **Diagram 1**, sew solid white 1½×3" rectangles to opposite edges of assorted print 3" square. Press seams toward rectangles.

2. Join solid white 1½×5" rectangles to remaining edges to make block center (**Diagram 2**); press as before.

Diagram 1   Diagram 2

3. Referring to **Diagram 3**, add remaining assorted print and solid white rectangles to block center to make block A. Press all seams away from center. Block A should be 13" square including seam allowances.

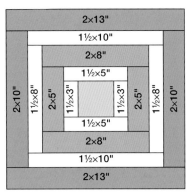

Diagram 3

Cut and Assemble Block B

The following instructions result in one block B. Repeat cutting and assembly steps to make 24 B blocks total.

From one assorted print, cut:
- 2—2×6" rectangles
- 2—2×3" rectangles

From a second assorted print, cut:
- 2—2×11" rectangles
- 2—2×8" rectangles

From solid white, cut:
- 2—1½×13" rectangles
- 2—1½×11" rectangles
- 2—1½×8" rectangles
- 2—1½×6" rectangles
- 1—3" square

1. Referring to **Diagram 4**, sew assorted print 2×3" rectangles to opposite edges of solid white 3" square. Press seams toward rectangles.

2. Join assorted print 2×6" rectangles to remaining edges to make block center (**Diagram 5**); press as before.

Diagram 4   Diagram 5

3. Referring to **Diagram 6**, add remaining solid white and assorted print rectangles to block center to make block B. Press all seams away from center. Block B should be 13" square including seam allowances.

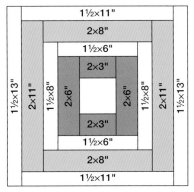

Diagram 6

Assemble Quilt Center

1. Referring to **Quilt Assembly Diagram**, lay out blocks in seven horizontal rows, alternating A and B blocks.

2. Sew together blocks in each row. Press seams in one direction, alternating direction with each row. Join rows to make quilt center; press seams in one direction. The quilt center should be 88" square including seam allowances.

Add Border

1. Cut and piece pink print 4½×42" strips to make a 4½×88" border strip.

2. Cut and piece yellow print 4½×42" strips to make a 4½×88" border strip.

Square Deal

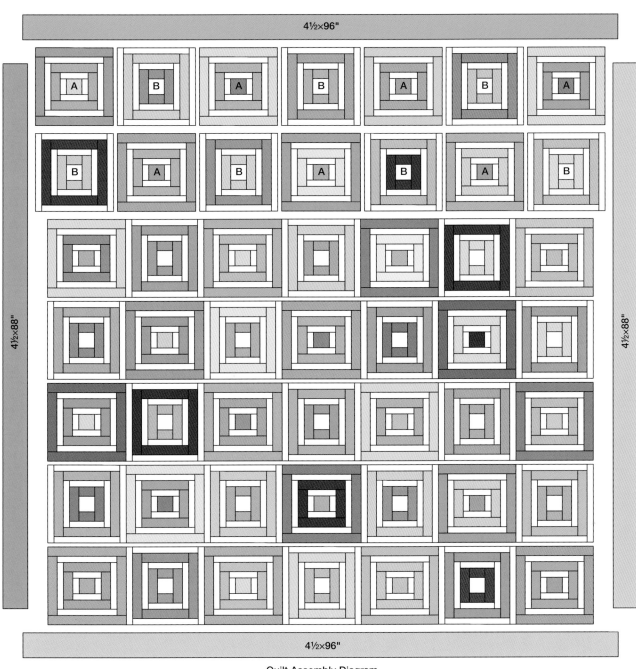

Quilt Assembly Diagram

3. Cut and piece blue print 4½×42" strips to make a 4½×96" border strip.

4. Cut and piece green print 4½×42" strips to make a 4½×96" border strip.

5. Referring to **Quilt Assembly Diagram**, sew pink print border strip and yellow print border strip to opposite edges of quilt center. Add blue print border strip and green print border strip to remaining edges to complete quilt top. Press all seams toward border.

continued

Finish Quilt

1. Layer quilt top, batting, and backing; baste. (For details, see Complete Quilt, *page 159.*)

2. Quilt as desired. Darlene Johannis machine-quilted a loop and star pattern across the entire quilt top.

3. Using diagonal seams, join assorted print 2½"-wide strips to make a 400"-long pieced binding strip. Bind with pieced binding strip. (For details, see Complete Quilt.)

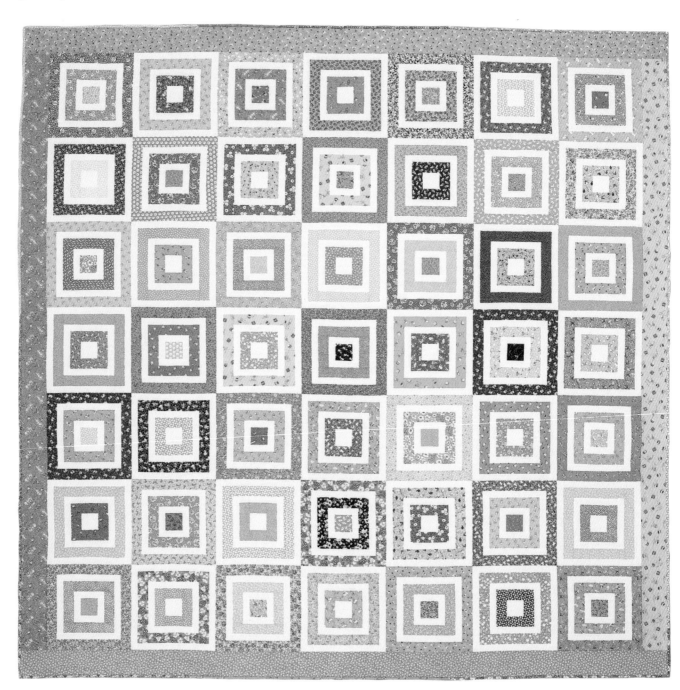

optional colors

Create an Illusion

Quilt tester Laura Boehnke used bright geometric prints for this striking two-color piece. "I only included A blocks in my version," Laura says, "so I turned every other block 90 degrees, resulting in seams that nest in the finished quilt." Changing the placement of the yellow and black fabric strips within the blocks increased the variety in the quilt and gives the illusion of blocks that appear to come toward you or recede.

STACKED WALL HANGING

Beautiful batiks create a serene effect on a quilted piece that

you can use to deck the hall or set the table.

Materials

⅝ yard dark purple batik (block centers, border,

   binding)

⅞ yard total assorted green, blue, and purple batiks

   (blocks)

1⅓ yards backing fabric

23×48" batting

Finished quilt: 17×42"

Cut Fabrics

Cut pieces in the order that follows in each section.

From dark purple batik, cut:
- 3—2½×42" binding strips
- 2—2½×38" border strips
- 2—2½×17" border strips

Cut and Assemble Block A

The following instructions result in one block A. Repeat cutting and assembly steps to make two A blocks total.

From dark purple batik, cut:
- 1—3" square
From one purple or blue batik, cut:
- 2—1½×5" rectangles
- 2—1½×3" rectangles
From one green or blue batik, cut:
- 2—2×8" rectangles
- 2—2×5" rectangles
From one green batik, cut:
- 2—1½×10" rectangles
- 2—1½×8" rectangles
From one blue batik, cut:
- 2—2×13" rectangles
- 2—2×10" rectangles

continued

1. Referring to Cut and Assemble Block A, *pages 99 and 100,* steps 1 and 2, use purple batik 3" square and purple or blue batik 1½×3" and 1½×5" rectangles to make block center.

Square Deal

2. Referring to Cut and Assemble Block A, Step 3, add remaining rectangles to block center to make block A.

Cut and Assemble Block B

From one green batik, cut:
- 1—3" square

From one purple batik, cut:
- 2—2×6" rectangles
- 2—2×3" rectangles

From a second green batik, cut:
- 2—1½×8" rectangles
- 2—1½×6" rectangles

From a second purple batik, cut:
- 2—2×11" rectangles
- 2—2×8" rectangles

From a third green batik, cut:
- 2—1½×13" rectangles
- 2—1½×11" rectangles

1. Referring to Cut and Assemble Block B, *page 100,* steps 1 and 2, use green batik 3" square and purple batik 2×3" and 2×6" rectangles to make block center.

2. Referring to Cut and Assemble Block B, Step 3, add remaining rectangles to block center to make one block B.

Assemble Quilt Top

1. Referring to photo at *left,* lay out blocks in a vertical row, placing block B in center. Sew together blocks to make quilt center. Press seams in one direction. The quilt center should be 13×38" including seam allowances.

2. Sew long dark purple batik border strips to long edges of quilt center. Add short dark purple batik border strips to remaining edges to complete quilt top. Press all seams toward border.

Finish Quilt

1. Layer quilt top, batting, and backing; baste. (For details, see Complete Quilt, *page 159.*)

2. Quilt as desired. This quilt is outline-quilted with three squares in each block.

3. Bind with dark purple batik binding strips. (For details, see Complete Quilt.)

FIVE-ROW THROW

Tame the lights and darks in 25 unique blocks within a thin brown frame.

Materials

⅜ yard brown tone-on-tone (inner border)

1½ yards red floral (outer border, binding)

1½ yards total assorted brown prints (blocks)

3 yards total assorted tan and tan-and-red prints (blocks)

1½ yards total assorted red prints (blocks)

4⅓ yards backing fabric

77" square batting

Finished quilt: 71" square

Cut Fabrics

Cut pieces in the order that follows in each section.

From brown tone-on-tone, cut:
• 7—1½×42" strips for inner border

From red floral, cut:
• 7—3½×42" strips for outer border
• 8—2½×42" binding strips

Cut and Assemble Red Blocks

The following instructions result in one red block. Repeat cutting and assembly steps to make 13 red blocks total.

From one brown print, cut:
• 1—3" square

From one tan or tan-and-red print, cut:
• 2—2×6" rectangles
• 2—2×3" rectangles

From one red print, cut:
• 2—1½×8" rectangles
• 2—1½×6" rectangles

From a second tan or tan-and-red print, cut:
• 2—2×11" rectangles
• 2—2×8" rectangles

From a second red print, cut:
• 2—1½×13" rectangles
• 2—1½×11" rectangles

1. Referring to Cut and Assemble Block B, *page 100,* steps 1 and 2, use brown print 3" square and tan or tan-and-red print 2×3" and 2×6" rectangles to make a block center.

2. Referring to Cut and Assemble Block B, Step 3, add remaining rectangles to block center to make a red block.

Cut and Assemble Brown Blocks

The following instructions result in one brown block. Repeat cutting and assembly steps to make 12 brown blocks total.

From one red print, cut:
• 1—3" square

From one tan or tan-and-red print, cut:
• 2—2×6" rectangles
• 2—2×3" rectangles

From one brown print, cut:
• 2—1½×8" rectangles
• 2—1½×6" rectangles

From a second tan or tan-and-red print, cut:
• 2—2×11" rectangles
• 2—2×8" rectangles

From a second brown print, cut:
• 2—1½×13" rectangles
• 2—1½×11" rectangles

1. Referring to Cut and Assemble Block B, *page 100,* steps 1 and 2, use red print 3" square and tan or tan-and-red print 2×3" and 2×6" rectangles to make block center.

2. Referring to Cut and Assemble Block B, Step 3, add remaining rectangles to block center to make a brown block.

Assemble Quilt Center

1. Referring to photo *opposite,* lay out blocks in five rows, alternating red and brown blocks; rotate each brown block 90 degrees so seams nest in finished quilt top, making construction easier.

2. Join blocks in each row. Press seams toward brown blocks. Join rows to make quilt center. Press seams in one direction. The quilt center should be 63" square including seam allowances.

Assemble Quilt Top

1. Cut and piece brown tone-on-tone 1½×42" strips to make:
• 2—1½×65" inner border strips
• 2—1½×63" inner border strips

2. Sew short inner border strips to opposite edges of quilt center. Join long inner border strips to remaining edges. Press all seams toward inner border.

3. Cut and piece red floral 3½×42" strips to make:
- 2—3½×71" outer border strips
- 2—3½×65" outer border strips

4. Sew short outer border strips to opposite edges of quilt center. Add long outer border strips to remaining edges to complete quilt top. Press all seams toward outer border.

Finish Quilt

1. Layer quilt top, batting, and backing; baste. (For details, see Complete Quilt, *page 159.*)

2. Quilt as desired. The featured quilt is stitched with an allover feather design.

3. Bind with red floral binding strips. (For details, see Complete Quilt.)

BUGGY *Wheels*

Simple squares and triangles form the "wheels" on this easy, single-block quilt from Buggy Barn designers Janet Nesbitt and Pam Soliday.

Materials

42—9×22" pieces (fat eighths) *or* 4⅔ yards total assorted dark prints (blocks, sashing)

12—⅜-yard pieces *or* 4⅝ yards total assorted light prints (blocks, sashing)

⅔ yard blue print (binding)

5⅛ yards backing fabric

76×93" batting

Finished quilt: 69½×86½"
Finished block: 16" square

Quantities are for 44/45"-wide, 100% cotton fabrics.
Measurements include ¼" seam allowances. Sew with right sides together unless otherwise stated.

Size options: For a chart of optional sizes, turn to *Pattern Sheet 1.*

Designer Notes

Sisters and designers Janet Nesbitt and Pam Soliday of The Buggy Barn in Reardan, Washington, used 42 dark prints and 12 light prints to achieve the desired scrappiness of their quilt. Use the total yardage as a guideline when selecting fabrics from your stash.

Cut Fabrics

Cut pieces in the following order.

From assorted dark prints, cut:
* 680—2⅞" squares
* 30—1½" sashing squares

From assorted light prints, cut:
* 49—1½×16½" sashing strips
* 360—2⅞" squares
* 240—2½" squares

From blue print, cut:
* 8—2½×42" binding strips

Assemble Triangle-Squares

1. Use a pencil to mark a diagonal line on wrong side of 520 assorted dark print 2⅞" squares.

2. Layer a marked dark print square atop each light print 2⅞" square. Sew each pair together with two seams, stitching ¼" on each side of drawn line (**Diagram 1**).

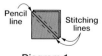

Diagram 1

To save time, chain-piece layered squares. To chain-piece, machine-sew pairs together one after the other without lifting the presser foot or clipping threads between pairs. First sew along one side of

continued

3. Cut a pair apart on drawn line to make two triangle units (**Diagram 3**). Press triangle units open to make two light-and-dark triangle-squares (**Diagram 4**). Each triangle-square should be 2½" square including seam allowances.

Diagram 3   Diagram 4

4. Repeat Step 3 to make 720 light-and-dark triangle-squares total.

5. Repeat steps 2 and 3 using remaining marked dark print 2⅞" squares and the 160 unmarked dark print 2⅞" squares to make 320 dark triangle-squares total.

Assemble Blocks

1. Referring to **Diagram 5**, lay out 36 light-and-dark triangle-squares, 16 dark triangle-squares, and 12 assorted light print 2½" squares in eight horizontal rows, noting direction of triangle-squares' seams.

Diagram 5

drawn lines, then turn group of pairs around and sew along other side of lines (**Diagram 2**). Clip connecting threads between pairs.

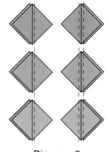

Diagram 2

2. Sew together pieces in each row. Press seams in one direction, alternating direction with each row.

3. Join rows to make a block; press seams in one direction. The block should be 16½" square including seam allowances.

4. Repeat steps 1–3 to make 20 blocks total.

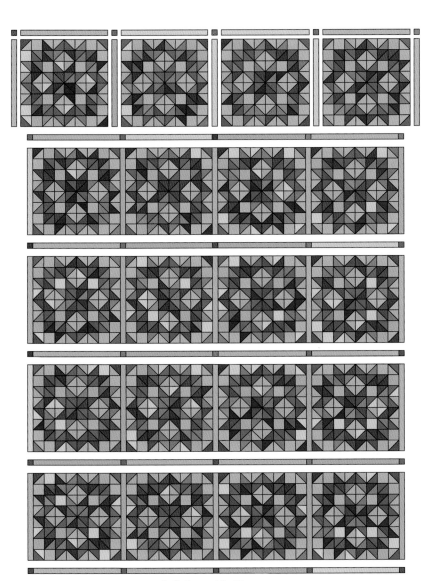

Quilt Assembly Diagram

Assemble Quilt Top

1. Referring to **Quilt Assembly Diagram**, lay out blocks, sashing strips, and sashing squares in 11 horizontal rows.

2. Sew together pieces in each row; press seams toward sashing strips. Join rows to complete quilt top. Press seams toward sashing rows.

Finish Quilt

1. Layer quilt top, batting, and backing; baste. (For details, see Complete Quilt, *page 159.*) Quilt as desired.

2. Bind with blue print binding strips. (For details, see Complete Quilt.)

optional colors

Bejeweled

A collection of jewel-tone prints inspired quilt tester Laura Boehnke to make this single-block wall hanging. "I emphasized the center star motif by surrounding it with a highly contrasting fabric," Laura says. "And to frame the piece, I chose a border print for the inner border that surrounds the sashing."

TWO-COLOR THROW

Some color combos never go out of style. Create a quilt that stands the test of time with classic blue and white prints.

Materials

- 2⅛ yards total assorted blue prints (blocks, sashing)
- 2¼ yards total assorted white-and-blue prints (blocks, sashing)
- 1½ yards navy blue print (border, binding)
- 3¾ yards backing fabric
- 67" square batting

Finished quilt: 60½" square

Cut Fabrics

Cut pieces in the following order.

From assorted blue prints, cut:
- 306—2⅞" squares
- 16—1½" sashing squares

From assorted white-and-blue prints, cut:
- 24—1½×16½" sashing strips
- 162—2⅞" squares
- 108—2½" squares

From navy blue print, cut:
- 6—4½×42" strips for border
- 7—2½×42" binding strips

Assemble Blocks

1. Use a pencil to mark a diagonal line on wrong side of 234 assorted blue print 2⅞" squares.

2. Referring to Assemble Triangle-Squares, steps 2 and 3, *pages 108 and 110,* use marked blue print squares and white-and-blue print 2⅞" squares to make 324 blue-and-white triangle-squares.

3. Referring to Assemble Triangle-Squares, steps 2 and 3, use remaining marked blue print squares and unmarked blue print 2⅞" squares to make 144 blue triangle-squares.

4. Referring to **Diagram 6,** lay out 36 blue-and-white triangle-squares, 16 blue triangle-squares, and 12 assorted white-and-blue print 2½" squares in eight horizontal rows. Referring to Assemble Blocks, steps 2 and 3, *page 110,* sew together pieces to make a block. Repeat to make nine blocks total.

Diagram 6

Assemble Quilt Top

1. Referring to photo *below,* lay out blocks, sashing strips, and sashing squares in seven rows. Sew together pieces in each row. Press seams toward sashing strips. Join rows to make quilt center; press seams toward sashing rows. The quilt center should be 52½" square including seam allowances.

2. Cut and piece navy blue print 4½×42" strips to make:
- 2—4½×60½" border strips
- 2—4½×52½" border strips

3. Sew short border strips to opposite edges of quilt center. Add long border strips to remaining edges to complete quilt top. Press all seams toward border.

Finish Quilt

1. Layer quilt top, batting, and backing; baste. (For details, see Complete Quilt, *page 159.*)

2. Quilt as desired. The featured quilt is stitched with an allover swirl pattern.

3. Bind with navy blue print binding strips. (For details, see Complete Quilt.)

STARRY WALL HANGING

Give your home a beachy, cottage look

with simplified stars.

Materials

⅛ yard total assorted light blue prints (blocks)

⅛ yard total assorted dark blue prints (blocks)

⅓ yard *each* of cream-and-blue and cream-and-pink prints (blocks)

⅛ yard total assorted light pink prints (blocks)

⅛ yard total assorted dark pink prints (blocks)

⅜ yard mottled light blue (sashing)

⅛ yard pink floral (sashing)

½ yard dark pink stripe (border)

¼ yard pink tone-on-tone (binding)

1 yard backing fabric

32×41" batting

Finished quilt: 25½×34½"
Finished block: 8" square

Cut Fabrics

Cut pieces in the following order.

From assorted light blue prints, cut:
• 11—2⅞" squares
From assorted dark blue prints, cut:
• 13—2⅞" squares
From cream-and-blue print, cut:
• 12—2⅞" squares
• 12—2½" squares
From assorted light pink prints, cut:
• 12—2⅞" squares
From assorted dark pink prints, cut:
• 12—2⅞" squares
From cream-and-pink print, cut:
• 12—2⅞" squares
• 12—2½" squares

From mottled light blue, cut:
- 17—1½×8½" sashing strips

From pink floral, cut:
- 12—1½" sashing squares

From dark pink stripe, cut:
- 2—3½×35½" border strips
- 2—3½×26½" border strips

From pink tone-on-tone, cut:
- 3—2½×42" binding strips

Assemble Triangle-Squares

1. Use a pencil to mark a diagonal line on wrong side of six assorted light blue print 2⅞" squares.

2. Referring to Assemble Triangle-Squares, steps 2 and 3, *pages 108 and 110,* use marked light blue print squares and assorted dark blue print 2⅞" squares to make 12 blue triangle-squares.

3. Mark a diagonal line on wrong side of cream-and-blue print 2⅞" squares. Referring to Assemble Triangle-Squares, steps 2 and 3, use marked squares and remaining light and dark blue print 2⅞" squares to make 14 dark blue-and-cream triangle-squares and 10 light blue-and-cream triangle-squares.

4. Mark a diagonal line on wrong side of six assorted light pink print 2⅞" squares.

5. Referring to Assemble Triangle-Squares, steps 2 and 3, use marked light pink print squares and assorted dark pink print 2⅞" squares to make 12 pink triangle-squares.

6. Mark a diagonal line on wrong side of cream-and-pink print 2⅞" squares. Referring to Assemble Triangle-Squares, steps 2 and 3, use marked squares and remaining light and dark pink print 2⅞" squares to make 12 light pink-and-cream triangle-squares and 12 dark pink-and-cream triangle-squares.

Assemble Blocks

1. Referring to **Diagram 7**, lay out four cream-and-blue print 2½" squares, four blue-and-cream triangle-squares, four light blue-and-cream triangle-squares, and four blue triangle-squares in four rows.

2. Sew together pieces in each row. Press seams in one direction, alternating direction with each row.

Join rows to make a blue block. Press seams in one direction. The block should be 8½" square including seam allowances.

3. Repeat steps 1 and 2 to make three blue blocks total (for one of the blue blocks, use six blue-and-cream triangle-squares and two light-blue-and-cream triangle-squares).

4. Using cream-and-pink print 2½" squares and dark pink-and-cream, light pink-and-cream, and pink triangle-squares, repeat steps 1 and 2 to make three pink blocks total.

Assemble Quilt Top

1. Referring to photo *opposite,* lay out blocks, sashing strips, and sashing squares in seven horizontal rows. Sew together pieces in each row. Press seams toward sashing strips. Join rows to make quilt center; press seams toward sashing rows. The quilt center should be 19½×28½" including seam allowances.

2. With midpoints aligned, sew short border strips to short edges of quilt center, beginning and ending seams ¼" from corners. Add long border strips, mitering corners, to complete quilt top. (For details, see Miter Borders, *page 158.*) Press all seams toward border.

Finish Quilt

1. Layer quilt top, batting, and backing; baste. (For details, see Complete Quilt, *page 159.*)

2. Quilt as desired. The blocks in this quilt are stitched with stylized loops in the star shapes and spirals in the cream backgrounds. The sashing strips feature wavy lines, and the border is quilted with echoing curls.

3. Bind with pink tone-on-tone binding strips. (For details, see Complete Quilt.)

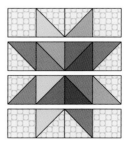

Diagram 7

SCRAPPY *Stars*

Bits and pieces of red, black, and ivory fabrics from her scrap bag and a love of traditional blocks inspired designer Carrie Nelson to create this stash-busting throw.

Materials

- 1½ yards total assorted ivory prints (blocks, inner border)
- 2½ yards total assorted black prints (blocks, inner border)
- 5¼ yards total assorted red prints (blocks, middle and outer borders)
- ⅔ yard black-and-red print (binding)
- 5⅛ yards backing fabric
- 79×91" batting

Finished quilt: 72½×84½"
Finished block: 6" square

Quantities are for 44/45"-wide, 100% cotton fabrics. **Measurements** include ¼" seam allowances. Sew with right sides together unless otherwise stated.

Designer Notes

When selecting fabrics for this quilt, designer Carrie Nelson decided the scrappier, the better. "While I didn't keep an exact count, I know that the finished quilt uses more than 60 different red fabrics, 35 different black fabrics, and 35 different ivory fabrics," she says.

Cut Fabrics

Cut pieces in the following order.

From assorted ivory prints, cut:
- 166—2⅞" squares
- 4—2½" squares

From assorted black prints, cut:
- 166—2⅞" squares
- 240—2½" squares

From assorted red prints, cut:
- 94—2½×6½" rectangles
- 2—2½×5½" rectangles
- 400—2½×4½" rectangles
- 4—2½×3½" rectangles
- 82—2½" squares
- 2—1½×2½" rectangles

From black-and-red print, cut:
- 8—2½×42" binding strips

Assemble Triangle-Squares

1. Use a pencil to mark a diagonal line on wrong side of each ivory print 2⅞" square.

2. Layer a marked ivory print square atop each black print 2⅞" square. Sew each pair together with two seams, stitching ¼" on each side of drawn line (**Diagram 1**).

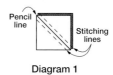

Pencil line

Stitching lines

Diagram 1

continued

3. Cut a pair apart on drawn line to make two triangle units (**Diagram 2**). Press each triangle unit open, pressing seam toward black triangle, to make two triangle-squares (**Diagram 3**). Each triangle-square should be 2½" square including seam allowances. Repeat to make 332 triangle-squares total.

Diagram 2

Diagram 3

Assemble Star Points

1. Use a pencil or dressmaker's chalk pencil to mark a diagonal line on wrong side of each black print 2½" square.

2. Align a marked black print 2½" square with one end of a red print 2½×4½" rectangle (**Diagram 4**; note direction of drawn line). Sew on drawn line. Trim excess, leaving ¼" seam allowance; press attached triangle open to make an A star point. The star point should be 2½×4½" including seam allowances. Repeat to make 120 A star points total.

3. Reversing direction of sewing line, repeat Step 2 to make a B star point (**Diagram 5**). Repeat to make 120 B star points total.

Diagram 4   Diagram 5

Assemble Blocks

1. Join a triangle-square and a red print 2½" square (**Diagram 6**). Press seam toward triangle-square.

2. Sew a red print 2½×4½" rectangle to bottom edge of Step 1 unit (**Diagram 7**). Press seam toward red print rectangle.

Diagram 6   Diagram 7

3. Lay out the Step 2 unit, an A star point, a B star point, and a triangle-square in two rows (**Diagram 8**). Sew together pieces in each row; press seams in direction of arrows. Join rows to make

a center block. To eliminate bulk where multiple seams come together, press seam open or follow designer Carrie Nelson's suggestion for pressing (see Tip, *below*). The block should be 6½" square including seam allowances.

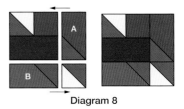

Diagram 8

4. Repeat steps 1–3 to make 80 center blocks total.

5. Repeat steps 2 and 3, using a red print 2½×4½" rectangle in place of the Step 1 unit, to make an outer block (**Diagram 9**). Repeat to make 40 outer blocks total.

Diagram 9

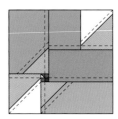

Diagram 10

TIP: *To reduce bulk where multiple seams meet, designer Carrie Nelson suggests removing a few stitches from the seam's intersection (see* inset*) so you can fan out the seam allowances and press them flat. When you look at the quilt top from the wrong side, the seams will be pressed in a clockwise direction* (**Diagram 10**).

Scrappy Stars

continued

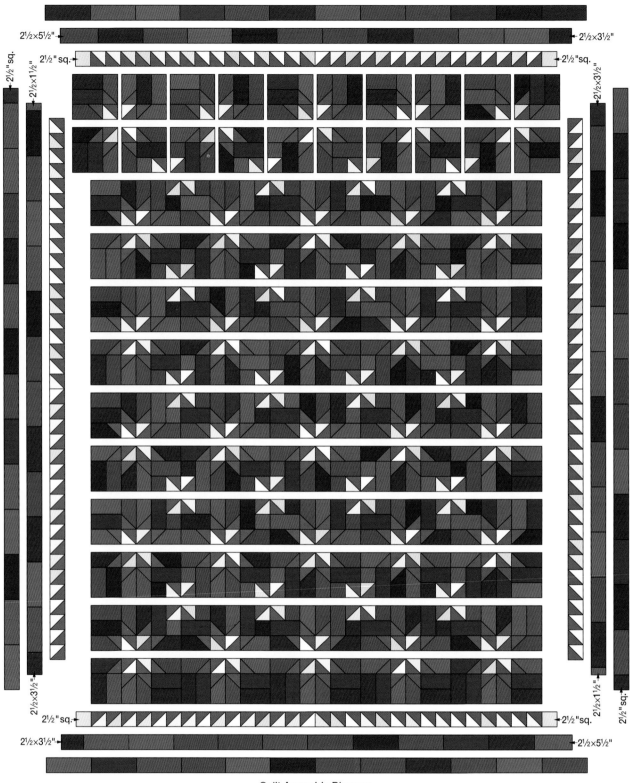

Labels around diagram:
2½x5½" 2½x3½"
2½"sq. 2½x1½" 2½"sq. 2½x3½"
2½"sq.
2½x3½"
2½x1½" 2½"sq.
2½"sq. 2½"sq.
2½x3½" 2½x5½"

Quilt Assembly Diagram

Assemble Quilt Center

1. With outer blocks surrounding center blocks, lay out blocks in 12 rows, paying attention to each block's rotation **(Quilt Assembly Diagram).**

2. Sew together blocks in each row. Press seams in one direction, alternating direction with each row.

Join rows to make quilt center. Block intersections (where the triangle-squares form pinwheels) will be bulky. Press seams open or follow Carrie's method of pressing. The quilt center should be 60½x72½" including seam allowances.

Assemble and Add Inner Border

1. Sew together 36 triangle-squares to make a long inner border strip (**Quilt Assembly Diagram**; note directions of triangle-square seams). Press seams toward ends of strip. The strip should be 2½×72½" including seam allowances. Repeat to make a second long inner border strip.

2. Join two assorted ivory print 2½" squares and 30 triangle-squares to make a short inner border strip. Press seams toward ends of strip. The strip should be 2½×64½" including seam allowances. Repeat to make a second short inner border strip.

3. Sew long inner border strips to long edges of quilt center. Sew short inner border strips to remaining edges. Press all seams toward quilt center. (Some seams on inner border strips will have been pressed in same direction as seams on quilt center. To prevent bulk, after Carrie pinned the border strips to the quilt center, she re-pressed seams in opposite directions as needed, then sewed border strips in place.)

Add Remaining Borders

Carrie offset the rectangles in middle and outer borders both to provide visual interest and so they would not align with seams on inner border. Unless otherwise indicated, red print rectangles on **Quilt Assembly Diagram** are 2½×6½".

1. Sew together a red print 2½×3½" rectangle, 12 assorted red print 2½×6½" rectangles, and a red print 1½×2½" rectangle to make a long middle border strip (**Quilt Assembly Diagram**). Press seams in one direction. The strip should be 2½×76½" including seam allowances. Repeat to make a second long middle border strip.

2. Sew together a red print 2½×5½" rectangle, 10 assorted red print 2½×6½" rectangles, and a red print 2½×3½" rectangle to make a short middle border strip (**Quilt Assembly Diagram**). Press seams in one direction. The strip should be 2½×68½" including seam allowances. Repeat to make a second short middle border strip.

3. Sew long middle border strips to long edges of quilt center. Sew short middle border strips to remaining edges. Press all seams toward middle border.

4. Sew together 13 assorted red print 2½×6½" rectangles and a red print 2½" square to make a long outer border strip. Press seams in one direction. The strip should be 2½×80½" including seam allowances. Repeat to make a second long outer border strip.

5. Sew together 12 assorted red print 2½×6½" rectangles to make a short outer border strip. Press seams in one direction. The strip should be 2½×72½" including seam allowances. Repeat to make a second short outer border strip.

6. Sew long outer border strips to long edges of quilt center. Sew short outer border strips to remaining edges to complete quilt top. Press all seams toward outer border.

Finish Quilt

1. Layer quilt top, batting, and backing; baste. (For details, see Complete Quilt, *page 159*.)

2. Quilt as desired. Machine-quilter Diane Tricka outline-quilted in the black points of the stars and in the inner border's triangle-squares (**Quilting Diagram**). She stitched small feathers in each star's triangle-squares and used an allover design in the red background. In the middle and outer borders, she stitched a large feather design.

3. Bind with black-and-red print binding strips. (For details, see Complete Quilt.)

Quilting Diagram

optional colors

Mint Julep and Rose

Using a combination of floral prints as the background, quilt tester Laura Boehnke mixed in red and pastel blue-green prints to create a soothing, fresh-as-spring wall hanging.

"By keeping the background prints light and making the stars from darker prints, the stars become more prominent in the finished quilt," Laura says. "Just as in the original quilt, I used the same prints as the stars for the sawtooth border to help frame the project and give it a cohesive appearance."

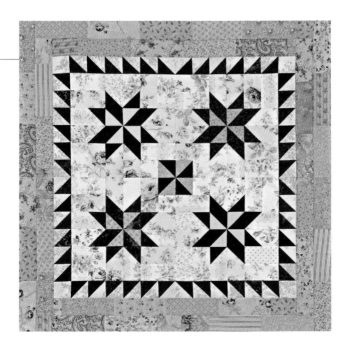

EMBROIDERED TABLECLOTH

Pieced borders and embroidery set the stage for a Thanksgiving feast.

Materials

2 yards mottled tan (tablecloth center,

    inner border)

½ yard total assorted green prints (inner border)

1⅛ yards total assorted rust and red prints

    (middle and outer borders)

3 yards backing fabric

Water-soluble marking pen

⅓ yard tear-away stabilizer

Machine-embroidery thread: tan

Finished tablecloth: 52×64"

Cut Fabrics

Cut pieces in the following order.

From mottled tan, cut:
- 1—40½×52½" rectangle
- 46—2⅞" squares
- 4—2½" squares

From assorted green prints, cut:
- 46—2⅞" squares

From assorted rust and red prints, cut:
- 64—2½×6½" rectangles
- 2—2½×6" rectangles
- 6—2½×5½" rectangles
- 2—2½×3" rectangles
- 2—1½×2½" rectangles

From tear-away stabilizer, cut:
- 6—3×15" rectangles

Embroider Tablecloth Center

The Full-Size Embroidery Pattern is on *Pattern Sheet 1*. If you have a computerized embroidery machine, instead of using the pattern, use your machine or embroidery software to make a "Give Thanks" design that is 1½" tall.

1. To make bottom guideline, measure and mark 13½" from bottom left corner of mottled tan 40½×52½" rectangle (red dot on **Quilt Assembly Diagram**, *page 124*). Beginning at mark, align ruler 1½" from bottom edge and use a water-soluble marking pen to lightly draw a 13½"-long bottom guideline. Repeat to make top guideline.

2. To make side guidelines, measure and mark 6¼"
from each corner (red dots on **Quilt Assembly
Diagram**). Beginning at one corner mark, align
ruler 1½" from side edge and lightly draw a 13½"-
long side guideline. Repeat with remaining corners
to make four side guidelines total.

3. Using a light table or sunny window, center
Embroidery Pattern along top guideline. Trace
pattern with water-soluble marking pen. Repeat
with bottom and side guidelines.

4. Pin or baste a stabilizer 3×15" rectangle to wrong
side of each traced area. Using tan embroidery
thread and a narrow stitch width, machine-satin-
stitch over traced patterns to make tablecloth
center. (Or use your embroidery machine to stitch
the design.)

Assemble and Add Inner Border
I. Use a pencil to mark a diagonal line on wrong
side of each mottled tan 2⅞" square.

2. Referring to Assemble Triangle-Squares, steps 2
and 3, *pages 117 and 118,* use marked mottled tan
squares and assorted green print 2⅞" squares to
make 92 triangle-squares total.

3. Referring to **Quilt Assembly Diagram**, *page 124,*
sew together 20 triangle-squares to make a short
inner border strip. Press seams toward green prints.
The short inner border strip should be 2½×40½"
including seam allowances. Repeat to make a
second short inner border strip.

4. Join 26 triangle-squares and two mottled tan
2½" squares to make a long inner border strip. Press
seams toward green prints. The long inner border
strip should be 2½×56½" including seam allowances.
Repeat to make a second long inner border strip.

5. Sew short inner border strips to short edges of
tablecloth center. Add long inner border strips to
remaining edges. Press seams toward inner border.

continued

Quilt Assembly Diagram

Scrappy Stars

strip should be 2½×60½" including seam allowances. Repeat to make a second long middle border strip.

3. Sew short middle border strips to short edges of tablecloth center. Add long middle border strips to remaining edges. Press all seams toward middle border.

4. Referring to **Quilt Assembly Diagram**, sew together seven assorted rust or red print 2½×6½" rectangles and two assorted rust or red print 2½×5½" rectangles to make a short outer border strip. Press seams in one direction. The short outer border strip should be 2½×52½" including seam allowances. Repeat to make a second short outer border strip.

5. Referring to **Quilt Assembly Diagram**, sew together nine assorted rust or red print 2½×6½" rectangles, one assorted rust or red print 2½×5½" rectangle, and one assorted rust or red print 1½×2½" rectangle to make a long outer border strip. Press seams in one direction. The long outer border strip should be 2½×60½" including seam allowances. Repeat to make a second long outer border strip.

6. Sew long outer border strips to long edges of tablecloth center. Add short outer border strips to remaining edges to complete tablecloth top. Press all seams toward outer border. The tablecloth top should be 52½×64½" including seam allowances.

Finish Tablecloth

1. Using backing fabric, make a 52½×64½" backing rectangle.

2. Layer tablecloth top and backing rectangle, right sides together; pin. Sew together along all edges, leaving a 6" opening along one edge for turning.

3. Turn tablecloth right side out through opening. Whipstitch opening closed. Press tablecloth flat.

4. To secure the layers together, stitch in the ditch between the tablecloth center and inner border. Press outer edges to complete tablecloth.

Assemble and Add Remaining Borders

Unless otherwise indicated, rust and red print rectangles on **Quilt Assembly Diagram** are 2½×6½".

1. Referring to **Quilt Assembly Diagram**, sew together six assorted rust or red print 2½×6½" rectangles, one assorted rust or red print 2½×6" rectangle, and one assorted rust or red print 2½×3" rectangle to make a short middle border strip. Press seams in one direction. The short middle border strip should be 2½×44½" including seam allowances. Repeat to make a second short middle border strip.

2. Sew together 10 assorted rust or red print 2½×6½" rectangles to make a long middle border strip. Press seams in one direction. The long middle border

STAIRSTEP CRIB QUILT

A diagonal pattern emerges from simple rectangles cut from small-scale florals.

Materials

⅓ yard *each* of blue floral, cream-and-blue print, green floral, two assorted blue prints, red print, and blue-and-red floral (blocks)

1½ yards red-and-orange floral (blocks, outer border, binding)

¼ yard *each* of white-and-red print, coral grid print, orange print, and red grid print (blocks)

⅓ yard solid red (inner border)

3 yards backing fabric

53×61" batting

Finished quilt: 46½×54½"
Finished block: 4" square

Cut Fabrics

Cut pieces in the following order.

From *each* of blue floral, cream-and-blue print, green floral, blue print Nos. 1–2, and red print, cut:
• 20—2½×4½" rectangles

From blue-and-red floral, cut:
• 19—2½×4½" rectangles

From red-and-orange floral, cut:
• 5—4½×42" strips for outer border
• 6—2½×42" binding strips
• 20—2½×4½" rectangles

From *each* of white-and-red print, coral grid print, and orange print, cut:
• 10—2½×4½" rectangles

From red grid print, cut:
• 9—2½×4½" rectangles

From solid red, cut:
• 5—1½×42" strips for inner border

continued

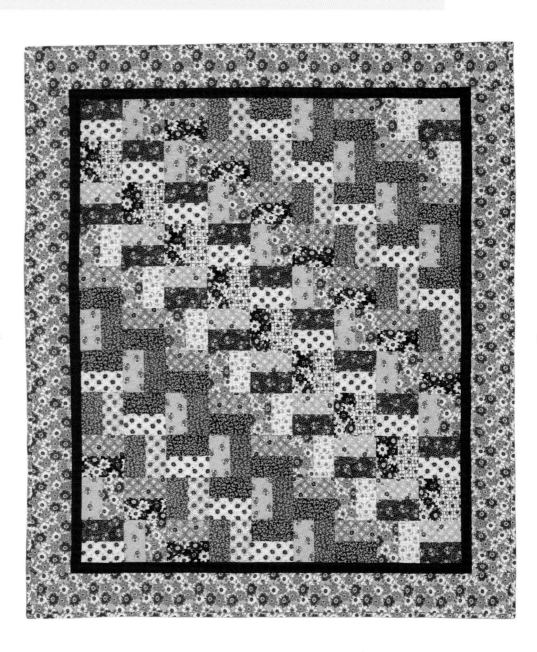

Assemble Blocks

1. Sew together a blue floral 2½×4½" rectangle and a cream-and-blue print 2½×4½" rectangle to make block A **(Diagram 11)**. Press seam toward darker print. Block A should be 4½" square including seam allowances.

Diagram 11

2. Repeat Step 1 to make 10 A blocks total.

3. Referring to **Quilt Assembly Diagram**, use the following rectangles and repeat Step 1 to make:
- 10 B blocks using green floral and red-and-orange floral
- 10 C blocks using blue print No. 1 and blue-and-red floral

- 10 D blocks using red print and white-and-red print
- 10 E blocks using blue print No. 2 and cream-and-blue print
- 10 F blocks using green floral and red print
- 10 G blocks using blue print Nos. 1 and 2
- 10 H blocks using red-and-orange floral and coral grid print
- 10 I blocks using orange print and blue floral
- 9 J blocks using blue-and-red floral and red grid print

Assemble Quilt Top

1. Referring to **Quilt Assembly Diagram**, lay out blocks in 11 horizontal rows; note direction of seams in blocks. Sew together pieces in each row. Press seams in one direction, alternating direction with each row. Join rows to make quilt center. Press seams in one direction. The quilt center should be 36½×44½" including seam allowances.

2. Cut and piece solid red 1½×42" strips to make:
- 2—1½×44½" inner border strips
- 2—1½×38½" inner border strips

3. Sew long inner border strips to long edges of quilt center. Add short inner border strips to remaining edges. Press all seams toward inner border.

4. Cut and piece red floral 4½×42" strips to make:
- 4—4½×46½" outer border strips

5. Sew outer border strips to long edges of quilt center. Add remaining outer border strips to remaining edges to complete quilt top. Press all seams toward outer border.

Finish Quilt

1. Layer quilt top, batting, and backing; baste. (For details, see Complete Quilt, *page 159*.)

2. Quilt as desired. This quilt features a flower-and-vine pattern in the quilt center and outer border, and continuous loops in the inner border.

3. Bind with red floral binding strips. (For details, see Complete Quilt.)

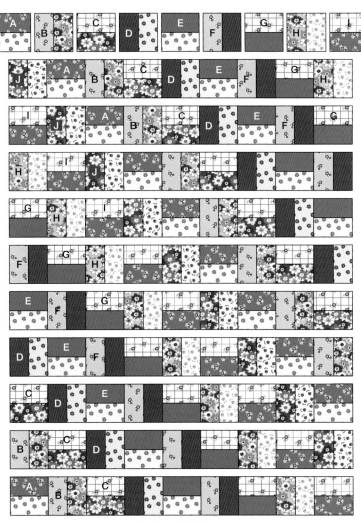

Quilt Assembly Diagram

Scrappy Stars

154

142

130

146

APPLIQUÉ
FOR EVERYONE

The endless possibilities of appliqué make it an

amazing skill for any quilter to have. Whether you're

a budding beginner or a seasoned pro, this chapter

offers a variety of projects that will help you get more

mileage from the basic techniques. Monogram a plush

pillow, add trendy embellishments to clothing, or fuse

flower appliqués to notecards.

AUTUMN *Bliss*

Enjoy the wonders of autumn year-round—without any raking.
Appliqué wool oak leaves and acorns, and hand-quilt to create designer
Lisa Bongean's stunning wall hanging.

Materials

1⅜ yards tan flannel (appliqué foundations, border)

3×10" piece dark red felted wool (star background appliqués)

½ yard dark green felted wool (circle and leaf appliqués)

2×6" piece dark gold felted wool (star appliqués)

5×10" piece black-and-brown-check felted wool (acorn top appliqués)

6×9" piece brown felted wool (acorn appliqués)

⅓ yard brown flannel (binding)

1¼ yards backing fabric

43" square batting

Lightweight fusible web

Perle cotton No. 12: olive green, brown, gold, dark red

Size 24 chenille needle

Finished quilt: 36½" square
Finished block: 10" square

Unless otherwise specified, **quantities** are for 44/45"-wide, 100% cotton fabrics. **Measurements** include ¼" seam allowances. Sew with right sides together unless otherwise stated.

Cut Fabrics

Cut pieces in the following order. Patterns are on *Pattern Sheet 1*.

To felt wool, machine-wash it in a hot-water-wash, cool-rinse cycle with a small amount of detergent; machine-dry on high heat and steam-press.

To use fusible web for appliquéing, complete the following steps.

1. Lay fusible web, paper side up, over patterns. Use a pencil to trace each pattern the number of times indicated in cutting instructions, leaving at least ¼" between tracings. Cut out each fusible-web shape roughly ⅛" outside traced lines.

2. Following manufacturer's instructions, press each fusible-web shape onto wrong side of designated wool; let cool. Cut out wool shapes on drawn lines. Peel off paper backings.

continued

From tan flannel, cut:
- 2—8½×36½" border strips
- 2—8½×20½" border strips
- 4—11" foundation squares

From dark red wool, cut:
- 4 of Pattern A

From dark green wool, cut:
- 16 of Pattern F
- 8 *each* of patterns G and G reversed
- 4 *each* of patterns B, H, and H reversed

From dark gold wool, cut:
- 4 of Pattern C

From black-and-brown-check wool, cut:
- 16 of Pattern D

From brown wool, cut:
- 16 of Pattern E

From brown flannel, cut:
- 4—2½×42" binding strips

Appliqué Blocks

1. Referring to **Full-Size Appliqué Placement Diagram** on *Pattern Sheet 1* and **Appliqué Placement Diagram**, arrange the following on a tan flannel foundation square: one dark red wool A piece, one dark green wool B circle, one dark gold

wool C star, four black-and-brown-check wool D acorn tops, four brown wool E acorns, and four dark green wool F leaves.

2. When you're pleased with the arrangement, fuse all pieces in place. (Because wool and flannel are so thick, to ensure a secure bond between appliqués and foundation, use a steam iron when fusing. Be careful not to scorch the wool; if desired, use a press cloth.)

3. Using matching perle cotton and a size 24 chenille needle, hand-blanket-stitch around each appliqué shape.

To blanket-stitch, pull needle up at A **(Blanket Stitch Diagram)**, form a reverse L shape with the floss, and hold angle of L shape in place with your thumb. Push needle down at B and come up at C to secure stitch. Continue in same manner around entire shape.

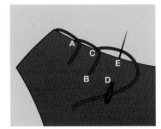

Blanket Stitch Diagram

4. Using olive green perle cotton, stem-stitch vein details in each F leaf.

To stem-stitch, pull needle up at A **(Stem Stitch Diagram)**. Insert needle back into fabric at B, ¼" away from A. Holding floss out of the way, bring needle back up at C and pull floss through so it lies flat against fabric. Pull gently with equal tautness after each stitch.

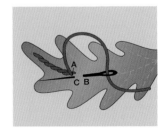

Stem Stitch Diagram

5. Centering the design, trim tan flannel foundation to 10½" square including seam allowances to make an appliquéd block.

Autumn Bliss

Appliqué Placement Diagram

6. Repeat steps 1–5 to make four appliquéd blocks total.

Assemble Quilt Top and Appliqué Border

1. Sew together appliquéd blocks in pairs. Press seams in opposite directions. Join pairs to make quilt center; press seam in one direction. The quilt center should be 20½" square including seam allowances.

2. Sew short tan flannel border strips to opposite edges of quilt center. Add long tan flannel border strips to remaining edges to complete quilt top. Press all seams toward border.

3. Referring to **Appliqué Placement Diagram**, lay out dark green wool G, G reversed, H, and H reversed leaves on border; fuse leaves in place.

4. Using olive green perle cotton, hand-blanket-stitch around each leaf, then stem-stitch vein details in each leaf.

Finish Quilt

1. Layer quilt top, batting, and backing; baste. (For details, see Complete Quilt, *page 159*.)

2. Quilt as desired. Designer Lisa Bongean started at the center of the wall hanging and used brown perle cotton No. 12 and a long stitch to hand-quilt diagonal lines about 1" apart **(Quilting Diagram)**. The resulting effect is a chevron pattern.

Quilting Diagram

3. Bind with brown flannel binding strips. (For details, see Complete Quilt.)

TIP: *To reinforce a primitive look on your wall hanging, stitch the hand-dyed wool appliqués in place with variegated perle cotton or embroidery floss. This will mimic the uneven color and mottled texture often present in hand-dyed wool.*

optional colors

Plaid Panache

The use of print fabrics sets quilt tester Laura Boehnke's version of *Autumn Bliss* apart from the original. "Don't be afraid to choose a strong print or plaid as the appliqué foundation," Laura says. Her appliqués in rich fall colors hold their own against a prominent gold-and-red homespun background. Laura machine-stitched around each fused appliqué with black thread for a folk art look.

PACKAGE TIE-ON

Give a simple gift that something extra by tying on embroidered wool shapes

that will last long after the package is opened.

Materials

2—6" squares brown felted wool (leaves)

4" square gold felted wool (acorn)

3" square dark brown felted wool (acorn top)

20" twine for wrapping package

Perle cotton No. 12: assorted browns to match

Size 24 chenille needle

Cut Fabrics

Cut pieces in the following order. This project uses *Autumn Bliss* patterns on *Pattern Sheet 1.*

To felt wool, machine-wash it in a hot-water-wash, cold-rinse cycle with a small amount of detergent; machine-dry on high heat; steam-press.

To use freezer-paper templates for cutting appliqué pieces, complete the following steps.

1. Lay freezer paper, shiny side down, over patterns. Use a pencil to trace each pattern the number of times indicated in cutting instructions, leaving ½" between tracings. Cut out freezer-paper shapes roughly ¼" outside drawn lines.

2. Using a hot, dry iron, press each freezer-paper shape, shiny side down, onto designated fabric; let cool. Cut out fabric shapes on drawn lines. Peel off freezer paper.

From *each* brown wool square, cut:
• 2 of Pattern G
From gold wool, cut:
• 2 of Pattern E
From dark brown wool, cut:
• 2 of Pattern D

Make Package Tie-On

1. Layer two matching brown wool G leaves. (Felted wool is reversible, so you can use either side for the right or wrong side.) Using matching perle cotton

and a size 24 chenille needle, repeat Appliqué Blocks, Step 3, *page 132,* to hand-blanket-stitch around leaf pair. Repeat to stitch around remaining leaf pair.

2. Using brown perle cotton, repeat Appliqué Blocks, Step 4, *page 132,* to stem-stitch vein details in each leaf pair.

3. Referring to photo *below,* position each dark brown wool D acorn top on a gold wool E acorn. Blanket-stitch across bottom edge of acorn top to join pieces. Layer pair of joined acorn pieces, and sew around edges with brown perle cotton and a blanket stitch.

4. Tie a knot at each end of twine. Stitch knot to back of each leaf. Sew acorn to top of one leaf to complete tie-on.

MONOGRAMMED PILLOW

An appliquéd initial and woodland motifs made from printed fabric combine

to make a modern-day family crest.

Materials

18×22" piece (fat quarter) brown print (appliqué foundation, pillow back)

2—6" squares assorted green prints (leaf appliqués)

2—4" squares assorted rust prints (acorn appliqués)

3" squares *each* of gold print, light brown print, and cream print (acorn top and circle appliqués)

4" square blue print (circle appliqué)

9×22" piece (fat eighth) mottled rust (monogram appliqué, piping)

Fusible web

Embroidery floss: olive green

1⅓ yards ¼"-diameter cording

Polyester fiberfill

Finished pillow: 10½" square

Cut Fabrics

Cut pieces in the following order. This project uses *Autumn Bliss* patterns on *Pattern Sheet 1*.

To use fusible web for appliquéing, complete the following steps. To make monogram letter pattern of your choice, select a font on your computer, enlarge to a height of 1¾", and print.

1. Lay fusible web, paper side up, over patterns. Use a pencil to trace patterns the number of times indicated in cutting instructions, leaving ½" between tracings. Cut out each fusible-web shape roughly ¼" outside traced lines.

2. Following manufacturer's instructions, press fusible-web shapes onto wrong sides of designated fabrics; let cool. Cut out fabric shapes on drawn lines. Peel off paper backings.

From brown print, cut:
- 1—10½" foundation square
- 1—10½" square for pillow back

From *each* green print, cut:
- 2 of Pattern F

From *each* rust print, cut:
- 2 of Pattern E

From *each* of gold and light brown print, cut:
- 2 of Pattern D

From cream print, cut:
- 1 of inside circle of Pattern B

From blue print, cut:
- 1 of outside circle of Pattern B

From mottled rust, cut:
- Enough 1¼"-wide bias strips to total 48" in length (For details, see Cut Bias Strips, *page 156*.)
- 1 of letter *S*

Appliqué Pillow Top

1. Referring to photo, *left,* arrange appliqué shapes on brown print 10½" foundation square. Fuse all pieces in place.

2. Using matching threads and working from bottom layer to top, machine-blanket-stitch around each appliqué shape.

3. Using two strands of olive green embroidery floss, backstitch stems and veins in each appliquéd leaf to complete pillow top.

To backstitch, bring needle up at A (**Backstitch Diagram**). Push needle down at B and come up at C. Continue in same manner.

Backstitch Diagram

Finish Pillow

1. Cut and piece mottled rust 1¼"-wide bias strips to make one long strip. Referring to Piping, Step 1, on *page 159,* prepare piping using bias strip.

2. Aligning raw edges and using a machine zipper foot, stitch piping to right side of pillow top, rounding corners slightly. (For details, see Piping, steps 2 and 3, on *page 159.*)

3. Pin brown print 10½" square pillow back to pillow top, aligning raw edges over piping. Using a machine zipper foot, sew together, leaving a 6" opening along one edge for turning.

4. Turn right side out and stuff with polyfill. Slip-stitch opening closed to complete pillow.

MEADOW
Blooms

Pretty pastel flowers blossom perennially on this simple wall quilt. Fusible appliqué makes this project from designer Cynthia Tomaszewski easy to complete.

Materials

¼ yard green print No. 1 (vine and stem appliqués)

¼ yard off-white print (appliqué foundations)

Scraps of assorted prints in pink, purple, yellow, and green (flower and leaf appliqués)

¼ yard yellow print (setting squares and triangles)

⅜ yard green print No. 2 (inner border, binding)

½ yard cream print (outer border)

⅞ yard backing fabric

30×36" batting

1½ yards lightweight fusible web

Embroidery floss: green, pink, purple, yellow

23—½"-diameter yellow buttons (flower centers)

Finished quilt: 23¾×29⅞"
Finished block: 4" square

Quantities are for 44/45"-wide, 100% cotton fabrics.
Measurements include ¼" seam allowances. Sew with right sides together unless otherwise stated.

Cut Fabrics

Cut pieces in the order that follows. Patterns are on *Pattern Sheet 1.* To use fusible web for appliquéing, complete the following steps.

1. Lay fusible web, paper side up, over patterns. Use a pencil to trace each pattern the number of times indicated in cutting instructions, leaving ½" between tracings. Cut out each fusible-web shape roughly ¼" outside traced lines.

2. Following manufacturer's instructions, press each fusible-web shape onto wrong side of designated fabric; let cool. Cut out fabric shapes on drawn lines. Peel off paper backings.

From green print No. 1, cut:
• Enough ½"-wide bias strips to total 130" in length for stem and vine appliqués (For details, see Cut Bias Strips, *page 156.*)
From off-white print, cut:
• 6—4½" foundation squares
From assorted pink prints, cut:
• 10 of Pattern H
• 9 of Pattern P
• 4 of Pattern O
• 1 *each* of patterns A, B, K, and L

continued

From assorted purple prints, cut:
- 6 of Pattern P
- 3 *each* of patterns E and F
- 1 of Pattern H

From assorted yellow prints, cut:
- 7 of Pattern H
- 3 of Pattern G

From assorted green prints, cut:
- 45 of Pattern Q
- 1 *each* of patterns C, D, I, J, M and N

From yellow print, cut:
- 2—7" squares, cutting each diagonally twice in an X for 8 setting triangles total (you will use 6)
- 2—4½" setting squares
- 2—3¾" squares, cutting each in half diagonally for 4 corner triangles total

From green print No. 2, cut:
- 3—2½×42" binding strips
- 2—1½×19⅜" inner border strips
- 2—1½×11¾" inner border strips

From cream print, cut:
- 2—5½×29⅜" outer border strips
- 2—5½×13¾" outer border strips

Appliqué Blocks

1. Cut and piece green print No. 1—½"-wide bias strips to make:
- 1—110"-long vine appliqué
- 1—3½"-long stem appliqué
- 1—3"-long stem appliqué
- 1—2¾"-long stem appliqué
- 2—2½"-long stem appliqués

2. Referring to photo, *opposite*, and **Full-Size Appliqué Placement Diagrams** on *Pattern Sheet 1*, arrange stem appliqués on three off-white print foundation squares; pin or baste in place. Turning under a ⅛" seam allowance, use small slip stitches and green thread to stitch stems in place.

3. Again referring to photo and **Full-Size Appliqué Placement Diagrams**, lay out flower and leaf appliqués on each off-white print foundation square; fuse in place.

4. Using two strands of matching embroidery floss, hand-blanket-stitch around each flower and leaf appliqué to make six appliquéd blocks.

To blanket-stitch, pull needle up at A (**Blanket Stitch Diagram**), form a reverse L shape with floss, and hold angle of L shape in place with your thumb. Push needle down at B and come up at C

to secure stitch. Continue in same manner, pushing needle down at D and up at E, to stitch around entire piece.

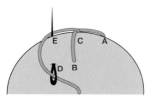

Blanket Stitch Diagram

5. Using two strands of green floss, stem-stitch vine tendrils on one appliquéd block as indicated on **Full-Size Appliqué Placement Diagrams.**

To stem-stitch, pull needle up at A (**Stem Stitch Diagram**). Insert needle into fabric at B, about ⅜" away from A. Holding floss out of the way, bring needle back up at C and pull floss through so it lies flat against fabric. Pull gently with equal tautness after each stitch.

Stem Stitch Diagram

Assemble Quilt Center

1. Referring to **Quilt Assembly Diagram**, lay out appliquéd blocks and yellow print setting squares and setting triangles in four diagonal rows.

Quilt Assembly Diagram

Meadow Blooms

2. Sew together pieces in each diagonal row. Press seams toward setting squares and triangles. Join rows; press seams in one direction.

3. Add yellow print corner triangles to make quilt center; press seams toward triangles. The quilt center should be 11¾×17⅞" including seam allowances.

Add Borders

1. Sew short green print No. 2 inner border strips to opposite edges of quilt center. Sew long green print No. 2 inner border strips to remaining edges. Press all seams toward inner border.

2. Sew short cream print outer border strips to short edges of quilt center. Join long cream print outer border strips to remaining edges to complete quilt top. Press all seams toward outer border.

Appliqué Border

1. Referring to photo for placement, arrange green print No. 1—110"-long vine appliqué on cream print outer border. Turning under a ⅛" seam allowance, use small slip stitches and green thread to stitch vine in place.

2. Lay out remaining flower and leaf appliqués along vine; fuse in place.

3. Using one strand of matching floss, blanket-stitch around each flower and leaf appliqué.

Finish Quilt

1. Layer quilt top, batting, and backing; baste. (For details, see Complete Quilt, *page 159.*)

2. Quilt as desired. Designer Cynthia Tomaszewski hand-quilted a 1"-wide diagonal grid across the quilt top.

3. Use three strands of yellow floss to sew a button on each flower center, tying thread tails on top of button.

To attach button, push needle down through one button hole, leaving a 3" thread tail. Bring needle back up through remaining hole; cut thread 3" above button. Tie thread tails in a knot to secure button. Trim thread tails to ¼".

4. Bind with green print No. 2 binding strips. (For details, see Complete Quilt.)

Meadow Blooms

FLORAL GREETING CARDS

Get more mileage from your patterns by fusing fabric appliqué shapes onto card stock notecards. Poke holes first with a paper piercer before stitching paper.

Materials for One 4×6" Card

14"-long piece lime green grosgrain ribbon

Scraps of pink, green, and purple prints (flower and leaf appliqués)

8×6" piece purple card stock

Glitter brad

Glue stick

Lightweight fusible web

Finished card: 4×6"

Cut Fabrics

Cut pieces in the following order. This project uses *Meadow Blooms* patterns on *Pattern Sheet 1*.

To use fusible web for appliquéing, complete the following steps.

1. Lay fusible web, paper side up, over patterns. Use a pencil to trace patterns the number of times indicated in cutting instructions, leaving ½" between tracings. Cut out each fusible-web shape roughly ¼" outside traced lines.

2. Following manufacturer's instructions, press fusible-web shapes onto wrong sides of designated fabrics; let cool. Cut out fabric shapes on drawn lines. Peel off paper backings.

From pink or green print, cut:
• 1 of Pattern P
From pink or purple print, cut:
• 1 of Pattern H
From green print, cut:
• 2 of Pattern Q

Appliqué Card

1. Loop lime green grosgrain ribbon around one short end of card stock 8×6" rectangle, 2½" from end. Center raw ends of ribbon on top of card stock rectangle and use glue stick to temporarily glue raw ends in place.

2. Referring to photo, *opposite,* arrange appliqué shapes on card stock, covering raw edges of ribbon. Fuse in place.

3. Using matching threads and working from bottom to top, machine-blanket-stitch in place.

4. Add glitter brad to center of flower. Fold appliquéd card stock rectangle in half to make a 4×6" card.

BATHROBE FOR HER

Using a double-appliqué method, stitch fashion-forward flowers to any clothing item.

Materials

Scraps of assorted pink and blue prints (flower appliqués)

12" square green print (stem and leaf appliqués)

Lightweight fusible web

5—½"-diameter buttons: white

Purchased bathrobe

Cut Fabrics

Cut pieces in the order that follows in each section. This project uses *Meadow Blooms* patterns on *Pattern Sheet 1.*

Make templates of flower patterns H and P. (For details, see Make and Use Templates, *page 156*.)

To use fusible web for appliquéing stem and Q leaf appliqués, complete the following steps.

1. Lay fusible web, paper side up, over Pattern Q. Use a pencil to trace pattern five times, leaving ½" between tracings. Cut out each fusible-web Q leaf roughly ¼" outside traced lines. Also cut a 1×15" strip of fusible web.

2. Position 1×15" fusible-web strip diagonally on wrong side of green print 12" square (so resulting strip will be cut on the bias.) Arrange fusible-web Q leaf pieces around 1×15" fusible-web strip. Following manufacturer's instructions, press. Let cool. Cut out fabric shapes on drawn lines. Peel off paper backings.

From green print, cut:
• 1—½×14"-long bias strip for stem appliqué
• 5 of Pattern Q

Cut Flower Appliqués

The flower appliqués are prepared using a double-appliqué method. This method eases the challenge of turning under seam allowances by facing the appliqué pieces with a matching piece of fabric. To use this method for cutting patterns H and P, complete the following steps.

1. Lay a template on wrong side of an assorted pink or blue print scrap. Use a pencil to trace around pattern. (This traced line will be your stitching line.)

2. Cut out fabric shapes, adding $\frac{3}{16}$" seam allowance beyond traced line.

From assorted pink and blue prints, cut:
• 10 *each* of patterns H and P

Prepare Flower Appliqués

1. Using a small stitch length, sew together two assorted pink or blue print P flowers on drawn line (**Diagram 1**).

2. Clip inner curves and points. Clip a small slit in center of one P flower, being careful not to cut through bottom fabric. Turn appliqué right side out through slit. Press P flower appliqué from right side.

3. Repeat steps 1 and 2 to prepare five P flower appliqués and five H flower appliqués total.

Diagram 1

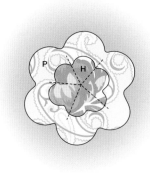

Diagram 2

Appliqué Robe

1. Referring to photo, *below,* position green print stem and leaf appliqués over shoulder of robe; fuse in place. Using matching thread and working from bottom layer to top, machine-blanket-stitch in place.

2. Layer a prepared H flower appliqué atop a prepared P flower appliqué. Position on robe over one end of stem appliqué. Referring to **Diagram 2**, machine-straight-stitch in place. Add a button in center of flower. Repeat to add a total of five H/P flower appliqués to robe shoulder area.

AUTUMN
Ambience

Designers Alma Allen and Barb Adams of

Blackbird Designs meld the rich, warm colors of fall with understated elegance

on a throw that combines delicate appliqué and classic piecing.

Materials

1¾ yards tan print No. 1 (blocks, border and

　　corner triangles)

4—½-yard pieces assorted red prints

　　(blocks, appliqués)

⅔ yard tan print No. 2 (blocks)

1¾ yards red floral (blocks, appliqués, binding)

3¼ yards backing fabric

58" square batting

Freezer paper

Fabric glue stick

Finished quilt: 51½" square
Finished block: 12" square

Quantities are for 44/45" wide, 100% cotton fabrics.
Measurements include ¼" seam allowances. Sew
with right sides together unless otherwise stated.

Cut Fabrics

Cut pieces in the following order. Patterns are on
Pattern Sheet 2.

　Designer Alma Allen uses a freezer-paper method
for machine appliquéing. The instructions that
follow are for this technique.

1. Lay freezer paper, shiny side down, over patterns.
Trace each pattern the number of times indicated
in cutting instructions. Cut out freezer-paper shapes
on drawn lines.

2. Using a hot, dry iron, press each freezer-paper
shape, shiny side down, onto wrong side of
designated fabric; let cool. Cut out each fabric
shape, adding a ³⁄₁₆" seam allowance to all edges.
Cut seam allowances slightly narrower at tips of
leaves; clip inner curves as necessary.

3. On each appliqué shape, run a glue stick along
seam allowance wrong side, then finger-press seam
allowance to back of freezer paper; let dry.

From tan print No. 1, cut:
- 2—18¼" squares, cutting each diagonally
  twice in an X for 8 setting triangles total
- 2—12½" squares
- 2—9⅜" squares, cutting each in half
  diagonally for 4 corner triangles total
- 10—4¼" squares, cutting each diagonally
  twice in an X for 40 small triangles total
- 40—2" squares

From assorted red prints, cut:
- 40—3⅞" squares, cutting each in half
  diagonally for 80 large triangles total
  (10 sets of eight matching triangles)
- 40—2½" squares (10 sets of four matching squares)
- 9—1×3" strips
- 3 *each* of patterns C, D, E, F, and H

continued

- 11 of Pattern A
- 12 of Pattern A reversed
- 31 of Pattern B
- 20 of Pattern B reversed
- 28 of Pattern K
- 18 of Pattern J
- 75 of Pattern G
- 6 of Pattern I

From tan print No. 2, cut:
- 1—12½" square
- 10—4¼" squares, cutting each diagonally twice in an X for 40 small triangles total
- 40—2" squares

From red floral, cut:
- 1—20" square, cutting it into enough 1"-wide bias strips to total 300" in length for vine and stem appliqués (For details, see Cut Bias Strips, *page 156*).
- 6—2½×42" binding strips
- 10—6½" squares
- 80—2" squares

Assemble Blocks

1. Referring to **Diagram 1**, join a tan print No. 1 small triangle to an assorted red print 2½" square. Note that a corner of the triangle will extend past edge of square. Press seam toward red print square.

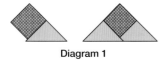

Diagram 1

2. Join a second tan print No. 1 small triangle to adjacent edge of red print square to make a triangle unit. Press seam toward red print square.

3. Referring to **Diagram 2**, sew matching red print large triangles to short edges of triangle unit to make a Flying Geese unit. Press seams toward red print triangles. The unit should be 6½×3½" including seam allowances.

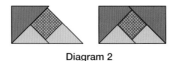

Diagram 2

4. Repeat steps 1–3 to make four matching Flying Geese units total.

5. Using tan print No. 1 or No. 2 small triangles, repeat steps 1–4 to make 10 sets total of four matching Flying Geese units.

6. Referring to **Diagram 3**, join two red floral 2" squares and two tan print No. 1—2" squares in pairs. Press seams toward red floral squares. Join pairs to make a Four-Patch unit. Press seam in one direction. The unit should be 3½" square including seam allowances. Repeat to make four matching Four-Patch units total.

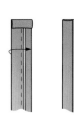

Diagram 3

7. Using red floral 2" squares and tan print No. 1 or No. 2—2" squares, repeat Step 6 to make 10 sets total of four matching Four-Patch units.

8. Sew together four matching Four-Patch units, four matching Flying Geese units, and a red floral 6½" square in rows **(Diagram 4)**. Press seams away from Flying Geese units. Join rows to make a star block. Press seams in one direction. The block should be 12½" square including seam allowances. Repeat to make 10 star blocks total.

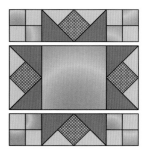

Diagram 4

Prepare Appliqués

1. Piece red floral 1"-wide bias strips to make one long strip. Fold strip in half lengthwise with wrong side inside; press. Sew together long edges, stitching a scant ¼" from edges **(Diagram 5)**. Trim seam allowance to ⅛". Refold strip, centering seam in back; press.

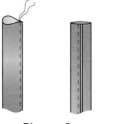

Diagram 5   Diagram 6

2. Cut prepared red floral bias strip to make:
- 8—15¼"-long vine appliqués
- 4—12"-long vine appliqués
- 6—7½"-long stem appliqués
- 6—5½"-long stem appliqués
- 9—3½"-long stem appliqués

3. Fold under ¼" at one short edge of each stem appliqué **(Diagram 6)**; press. Fold strip in half lengthwise; press. (Do not fold vine appliqués in half—they will be twice as wide as the stem appliqués.)

4. Prepare nine assorted red print 1×3" strips in the same manner as Step 1 to make appliqué strips. (Three of these strips are used to make the snowflake-style flower in each appliquéd block.) Referring to **Diagram 7**, make a ⅜"-long cut in center of short edges of each prepared red print appliqué strip.

3/8"

Diagram 7

continued

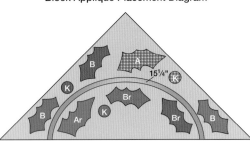

Block Appliqué Placement Diagram

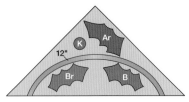

Setting Triangle
Appliqué Placement Diagram

Corner Triangle
Appliqué Placement Diagram

Quilting Diagram

Appliqué Blocks and Triangles

1. Fold each tan print Nos. 1 and 2—12½" square in half diagonally twice. Lightly finger-press each fold to create three foundation squares with appliqué placement guidelines; unfold.

2. Referring to **Full-Size Block Appliqué Placement Diagram** on *Pattern Sheet 2* and **Block Appliqué Placement Diagram**, lay out two red floral 7½"-long stem appliqués, two red floral 5½"-long stem appliqués, three red floral 3½"-long stem appliqués, three red print 3"-long appliqué strips, and remaining appliqué pieces on each tan print foundation square; baste in place.

3. Using red thread and working from bottom layer to top, machine-appliqué pieces in place to make three appliquéd blocks total. Tip: If residue from the glue stick used to prepare your appliqué pieces builds up on your needle while machine-appliquéing, wipe it off with rubbing alcohol.

4. Referring to **Full-Size Setting Triangle Appliqué Placement Diagram** on *Pattern Sheet 2* and **Setting Triangle Appliqué Placement Diagram**, lay out one red floral 15¼"-long vine appliqué and remaining appliqué pieces on a tan print No. 1 setting triangle. Baste and machine-appliqué as before to make an appliquéd setting triangle. Repeat to make eight appliquéd setting triangles total.

5. Referring to **Full-Size Corner Triangle Appliqué Placement Diagram** on *Pattern Sheet 2* and **Corner Triangle Appliqué Placement Diagram**, lay out one red floral 12"-long vine appliqué and remaining appliqué pieces on a tan print No. 1 corner triangle. Baste and machine-appliqué as before to make an appliquéd corner triangle. Repeat to make four appliquéd corner triangles total.

6. Soak appliquéd blocks, setting triangles, and corner triangles in cold water to remove glue. Trim excess foundation fabric from behind appliqués, leaving ¼" seam allowances. Peel away freezer paper and discard. Use dry towel to remove excess water, then air-dry; press blocks and triangles from wrong side.

Assemble Quilt Top

1. Referring to **Quilt Assembly Diagram**, lay out star blocks, appliquéd blocks, and appliquéd setting triangles in five diagonal rows.

Quilt Assembly Diagram

2. Sew together pieces in each row. Press seams in one direction, alternating direction with each row. Join rows; press seams in one direction.

3. Add appliquéd corner triangles to complete quilt top. Press seams toward triangles.

Finish Quilt

1. Layer quilt top, batting, and backing; baste. (For details, see Complete Quilt, *page 159.*)

2. Quilt as desired. Machine-quilter Jeanne Zyck outline-quilted each appliqué piece in the blocks, setting triangles, and corner triangles **(Quilting Diagram).** She added veins to the appliquéd leaves and decorative lines to the red print F flowers and H vases. She stitched a different leaf-and-vine design in the red floral center squares, red print 2½" squares, and red print large triangles. She quilted a curved outline in each square of the Four-Patch units and in each tan print triangle of the Flying Geese units.

3. Bind with red floral binding strips. (For details, see Complete Quilt.)

IN-BLOOM WALL HANGING

Broaden your palette, and surround an appliquéd bouquet with multicolor blocks.

Materials

5" square *each* navy blue, brown, red, and olive green print (star blocks)

½ yard cream print (star blocks, appliqué foundation)

4—10" squares assorted black prints (star blocks)

⅓ yard large black floral (star blocks)

18×22" piece (fat quarter) green print (stem appliqués)

Scraps of assorted red, blue, black, brown, and green prints (appliqués)

⅝ yard gold print (setting and corner triangles)

⅓ yard solid black (binding)

1¼ yards backing fabric

41" square batting

Lightweight fusible web

Finished quilt: 34½" square

Cut Fabrics

Cut pieces in the order that follows. This project uses *Autumn Ambience* patterns and one additional pattern, all on *Pattern Sheet 2.*

To use the fusible web for appliquéing, complete the following steps.

I. Lay fusible web, paper side up, over patterns. Use a pencil to trace patterns the number of times indicated in cutting instructions, leaving ½" between tracings. Cut out each fusible-web shape roughly ¼" outside traced lines.

2. Following manufacturer's instructions, press fusible-web shapes onto wrong sides of designated fabrics; let cool. Cut out fabric shapes on drawn lines. Peel off paper backings.

From *each* of the navy blue, brown, red, and olive green prints, cut:
- 4—2½" squares

From cream print, cut:
- 1—12½" foundation square
- 8—4¼" squares, cutting each diagonally twice in an X for 32 small triangles total
- 32—2" squares

From *each* assorted black print, cut:
- 4—3⅞" squares, cutting each in half diagonally for 8 large triangles total

From large black floral, cut:
- 4—6½" squares
- 32—2" squares

From green print, cut:
- Enough 1"-wide bias strips to total 40" in length for stem appliqués (For details, see Cut Bias Strips, *page 156.*)

From assorted red, blue, black, brown, and green prints, cut:
- 1 *each* of patterns A, B, C, D, E, F, H, and L
- 22 of Pattern G
- 6 of Pattern J
- 2 of Pattern I

From gold print, cut:
- 1—18¼" square, cutting it diagonally twice in an X for 4 setting triangles total
- 2—9⅜" squares, cutting each in half diagonally for 4 corner triangles total

From solid black, cut:
- 4—2½×42" binding strips

Assemble Star Blocks

I. Using navy blue print 2½" squares, cream print small triangles, and matching black print large triangles, repeat Assemble Blocks, steps 1–3, *page 148,* to make four blue Flying Geese units.

2. Using brown, red, and olive green print 2½" squares, repeat Step 1 to make four sets total of four matching Flying Geese units.

3. Using large black floral 2" squares and cream print 2" squares, repeat Assemble Blocks, Step 6, *page 148,* to make 16 Four-Patch units total.

4. Using a large black floral 6½" square and units just made, repeat Assemble Blocks, Step 8, *page 148,* to make a star block. Repeat to make four star blocks total.

Appliqué Block

I. Piece green print 1"-wide bias strips to make one 40"-long strip. Referring to Prepare Appliqués, Step 1, *page 148,* prepare 40"-long strip. Cut prepared strip to make:
- 2—7½"-long stem appliqués
- 2—5½"-long stem appliqués
- 3—3½"-long stem appliqués

2. Referring to Appliqué Blocks and Triangles, steps 1–3, *page 150,* appliqué one block. (Use Pattern L instead of 3"-long appliqué strips, and fuse all pieces in place.)

Assemble Quilt Top

Referring to photo, *opposite,* lay out star blocks, appliquéd block, and setting triangles in diagonal rows. Sew together pieces in each row. Press seams toward setting triangles and appliqué block. Join rows; press seams in one direction. Add four gold print corner triangles to complete quilt top. Press seams toward corner triangles.

Finish Quilt

I. Layer quilt top, batting, and backing; baste. (For details, see Complete Quilt, *page 159.*) Quilt as desired.

2. Bind with solid black binding strips. (For details, see Complete Quilt.)

COOL BLUE BATIK QUILT

Cream print setting squares allow the dreamy blue batiks

to turn heads on this peaceful throw.

Materials

6—18×22" pieces (fat quarters) assorted blue

    batiks and prints (star blocks, appliqués)

2 yards cream print (star blocks, border

    and corner triangle appliqué foundations,

    setting squares)

1½ yards blue-and-tan batik (star blocks,

    appliques, binding)

3¼ yards backing fabric

58" square batting

Lightweight fusible web

Finished quilt: 51½" square

Cut Fabrics

Cut pieces in the following order. This project uses *Autumn Ambience* patterns on *Pattern Sheet 2*.

To use fusible web for appliquéing, complete the following steps.

1. Lay fusible web, paper side up, over patterns. Use a pencil to trace patterns the number of times indicated in cutting instructions, leaving ½" between tracings. Cut out each fusible-web shape roughly ¼" outside traced lines.

2. Following manufacturer's instructions, press fusible-web shapes onto wrong sides of designated fabrics; let cool. Cut out fabric shapes on drawn lines. Peel off paper backings.

From assorted blue batiks and prints, cut:
- 40—3⅞" squares, cutting each in half diagonally for 80 large triangles total (10 sets of eight matching triangles)
- 40—2½" squares (10 sets of four matching squares)
- 20 of Pattern A
- 48 of Pattern B
- 28 of Pattern K
- 16—2" squares (2 sets of eight matching squares)

From cream print, cut:
- 2—18¼" squares, cutting each diagonally twice in an X for 8 setting triangles total
- 3—12½" setting squares
- 2—9⅜" squares, cutting each in half diagonally for 4 corner triangles total
- 20—4¼" squares, cutting each diagonally twice in an X for 80 small triangles total
- 64—2" squares

From blue-and-tan batik, cut:
- 6—2½×42" binding strips
- 1—16" square, cutting it into enough 1"-wide bias strips to total 170" in length for vine appliqués (For details, see Cut Bias Strips, *page 156.*)
- 10—6½" squares
- 80—2" squares

Assemble Star Blocks

1. Using matching blue batik or print 2½" squares, cream print small triangles, and matching blue batik or print large triangles, repeat Assemble Blocks, steps 1–3, *page 148,* to make four matching Flying Geese units.

2. Repeat Step 1 to make 10 sets total of four matching Flying Geese units.

3. Using blue-and-tan batik 2" squares and cream print 2" squares, repeat Assemble Blocks, Step 6, *page 148,* to make 32 Four-Patch units. Using blue batik or print squares instead of cream print, make eight Four-Patch units (two sets of four matching).

4. Using a blue-and-tan batik 6½" square four matching Flying Geese units, and four matching Four-Patch units, repeat Assemble Blocks, Step 8, *page 148,* to make a star block. Repeat to make 10 star blocks total.

Appliqué Triangles

1. Piece blue-and-tan batik 1"-wide bias strips to make one 170"-long strip. Referring to Prepare Appliqués, Step 1, *page 148,* prepare 170"-long strip. Cut prepared strip to make:
- 8—15¼"-long vine appliqués
- 4—12"-long vine appliqués

2. Referring to Appliqué Blocks and Triangles, steps 4 and 5, *page 150,* appliqué eight setting triangles and four corner triangles, fusing pieces in place.

Assemble Quilt Top

Referring to Assemble Quilt Top, *page 150,* sew together star blocks, cream print setting squares, appliquéd setting triangles, and appliquéd corner triangles to make quilt top.

Finish Quilt

1. Layer quilt top, batting, and backing; baste. (For details, see Complete Quilt, *page 159.*) Quilt as desired.

2. Bind with blue-and-tan batik binding strips. (For details, see Complete Quilt.)

QUILTER'S SCHOOLHOUSE

Refer to these tips and techniques when making your projects.

CHOOSE FABRICS

The best fabric for quiltmaking is 100% cotton because it minimizes seam distortion, presses crisply, and is easy to quilt. Unless otherwise noted, quantities in Materials lists are for 44/45"-wide fabrics. We call for a little extra yardage to allow for minor errors and slight shrinkage.

CUT BIAS STRIPS

Strips for curved appliqué pattern pieces, such as meandering vines, and for binding curved edges should be cut on the bias, which runs at a 45° angle to the selvages of a woven fabric and has the most give or stretch.

To cut bias strips, begin with a fabric square or rectangle. Use a large acrylic ruler to square up the left edge of the fabric. Then make a cut at a 45° angle to the left edge (**Bias Strip Diagram**). Handle the diagonal edges carefully to avoid distorting the bias. To cut a strip, measure the desired width parallel to the 45° cut edge; cut. Continue cutting enough strips to total the length needed.

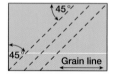

Bias Strip Diagram

MAKE AND USE TEMPLATES
Make Templates

A template is a pattern made from extra-sturdy material so you can trace around it many times without wearing away the edges. Acrylic templates for many common shapes are available at quilt shops. Or make your own templates by duplicating printed patterns (such as those on the Pattern Sheets) onto template plastic.

To make permanent templates, we recommend using easy-to-cut template plastic. This material lasts indefinitely, and its transparency allows you to trace the pattern directly onto its surface.

To make a template, lay the plastic over a printed pattern. Trace the pattern onto the plastic using a ruler and a permanent marker to ensure straight lines, accurate corners, and permanency.

For hand piecing and appliqué, make templates the exact size the finished pieces will be (without seam allowances). For hand piecing, this means tracing the patterns' dashed lines.

For machine piecing, make templates that include seam allowances by tracing the patterns' solid and dashed lines.

For easy reference, mark each template with its letter designation, grain line (if noted on the pattern), and block name. Cut out the traced shapes on their outer lines. Verify each template's shape and size by placing it over its printed pattern. Templates must be accurate because errors, however small, will compound many times as you assemble a quilt. To check the templates' accuracy, make a test block before cutting the fabric pieces for an entire quilt.

Use Templates

To trace a template on fabric, use a pencil, a white dressmaker's pencil, chalk, or a special fabric marker that makes a thin, accurate line. Do not use a ballpoint or ink pen; it may bleed if washed. Test all marking tools on a fabric scrap before using them.

To make pieces for hand piecing or appliqué, place a template facedown on the wrong side of the fabric and trace. Then reposition the template at least $1/2$" away from the previous tracing, trace again, and repeat (**Diagram 1**). The lines you trace on the fabric are sewing lines. Mark cutting lines $1/4$" away from the sewing lines, or estimate the distance by eye when cutting out the pieces with scissors. For hand piecing, add a $1/4$" seam allowance; for hand appliqué, add a $3/16$" seam allowance.

Because templates used to make pieces for machine piecing have seam

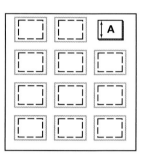

Diagram 1

allowances included, you can use common tracing lines for efficient cutting. Place a template facedown on the wrong side of the fabric, and trace. Then reposition the template without a space between it and the previous tracing, trace again, and repeat (**Diagram 2**). Using a rotary cutter and ruler, cut out pieces, cutting precisely on the drawn lines.

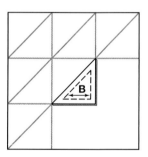

Diagram 2

Templates for Angled Pieces

When two patchwork pieces come together and form an angled opening, a third piece must be set into this angle. This happens frequently when using diamond shapes.

For a design that requires setting in, a pinhole or window template makes it easy to mark the fabric with each shape's exact sewing and cutting lines and the exact point of each corner on the sewing line. By matching the corners of adjacent pieces, you'll be able to sew them together easily and accurately.

To make a pinhole template, lay template plastic over a pattern piece. Trace both the cutting and sewing lines onto the plastic. Carefully cut out the template on the cutting line. Using a sewing-machine needle or any large needle, make a hole in the template at each corner on the sewing line (matching points). The holes must be large enough for a pencil point or other fabric marker to poke through.

Trace Angled Pieces

To mark fabric using a pinhole template, lay it facedown on the wrong side of the fabric, and trace. Using a pencil, mark dots on the fabric through the holes in the template to create matching points; then cut out the fabric piece on the drawn line.

To mark fabric using a window template, lay it facedown on the wrong side of the fabric (**Diagram 3**). With a marking tool, mark the cutting line, sewing line, and each corner on the sewing line (matching points). Cut out the fabric piece on the cutting lines, making sure all pieces have sewing lines and matching points marked.

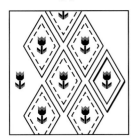

Diagram 3

PLAN FOR CUTTING

Quilt-Lovers' Favorites® instructions list pieces in the order they should be cut to make the best use of your fabrics.

Always consider the fabric grain before cutting. The arrow on a pattern piece indicates which direction the grain should run. One or more straight sides of a pattern piece should follow the fabric's lengthwise or crosswise grain.

The lengthwise grain, parallel to the selvages (the tightly finished edges), has the least amount of stretch. The crosswise grain, perpendicular to the selvages, has a little more give. The edge of any pattern piece that will be on the outside of a block or quilt should always be cut on the lengthwise grain. Do not use the selvages of a woven fabric in a quilt. When washed, it may shrink more than the rest of

the fabric. Be sure to press the fabric before cutting to remove any wrinkles or folds.

In projects larger than 42" in length or width, we usually specify that the border strips be cut the width (crosswise grain) of the fabric and pieced to use the least amount of fabric. If you'd prefer to cut the border strips on the lengthwise grain and not piece them, you'll need to refigure the yardage.

PIECING
Hand Piecing

In hand piecing, seams are sewn only on the marked sewing lines; the seam allowances remain unstitched. Begin by matching the edges of two pieces with the fabrics' right sides together. Sewing lines should be marked on the wrong side of each piece. Push a pin through both fabric layers at each corner (**Diagram 4**). Secure the pins perpendicular to the sewing line. Insert more pins between the corners.

Insert a needle through both fabrics at the seam-line corner. Make one or two backstitches atop the first stitch to secure the thread. Weave the needle in and out of the fabric along the seam line, taking four to six tiny stitches at a time before you pull the thread taut (**Diagram 5**). Remove the pins as you sew. Turn the work over occasionally to see that the stitching follows the marked sewing line on the other side.

Diagram 4   Diagram 5

Sew eight to 10 stitches per inch along the seam line. At the end of the seam, remove the last pin and make the ending stitch through the hole left by the corner pin. Backstitch over the last stitch and end the seam with a loop knot (**Diagram 6**).

Diagram 6

To join rows of patchwork by hand, hold the sewn pieces with right sides together and seams matched. Insert pins at the corners of the matching pieces. Add additional pins as necessary, securing each pin perpendicular to the sewing line (**Diagram 7**).

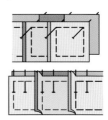

Diagram 7

Stitch the joining seam as before, but do not sew across the seam allowances that join the patches. At each seam allowance, make a backstitch or loop knot; then slide the needle through the seam allowance (**Diagram 8**). Knot or backstitch again to give the intersection strength; then sew the remainder of the seam. Press each seam as it is completed.

Diagram 8

Machine Piecing

Machine piecing depends on sewing an exact ¼" seam allowance. Some machines have a presser foot that is the proper width, or a ¼" foot is available. To check the width of a machine's presser foot, sew a sample seam with the raw fabric edges aligned with the right edge of the presser foot; measure the resultant seam allowance using graph paper with a ¼" grid.

Using two thread colors—one in the needle and one in the bobbin—can help you to better match your thread color to your fabrics. If your quilt has many fabrics, use a neutral color, such as gray or beige, for both the top and bobbin threads throughout the quilt.

Press for Success

In quilting, almost every seam needs to be pressed before the piece is sewn to another, so keep your iron and

continued

ironing board near your sewing area. It's important to remember to press with an up-and-down motion. Moving the iron around on the fabric can distort seams, especially those sewn on the bias.

Project instructions in this book generally tell you in what direction to press each seam. When in doubt, press the seam allowance toward the darker fabric. When joining rows of blocks, alternate the direction the seam allowances are pressed to ensure flat corners.

Set in Pieces

The key to sewing angled pieces together is aligning marked matching points carefully. Whether you're stitching by machine or hand, start and stop sewing precisely at the matching points (see dots in **Diagram 9**, top) and backstitch to secure the ends of the seams. This prepares the angle for the next piece to be set in.

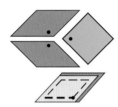

Diagram 9

Join two diamond pieces, sewing between matching points to make an angled unit (**Diagram 9**).

Follow the specific instructions for either machine or hand piecing to complete the set-in seam.

MACHINE PIECING

With right sides together, pin one piece of the angled unit to one edge of the square (**Diagram 10**). Match the seam's matching points by pushing a pin through both fabric layers to check the alignment. Machine-stitch the seam between the matching points. Backstitch to secure the ends of the seam; do not stitch into the $1/4$" seam allowance. Remove the unit from the sewing machine.

Diagram 10

Bring the adjacent edge of the angled unit up and align it with the next edge of the square (**Diagram 11**). Insert a pin in each corner to align matching points; then pin the remainder of the seam. Machine-stitch between matching points as before. Press the seam allowances of the set-in piece away from it.

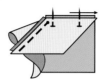

Diagram 11

HAND PIECING

Pin one piece of the angled unit to one edge of the square with right sides together (**Diagram 12**). Use pins to align matching points at the corners.

Hand-sew the seam from the open end of the angle into the corner. Remove pins as you sew between matching points. Backstitch at the corner to secure stitches. Do not sew into the $1/4$" seam allowance, and do not cut your thread.

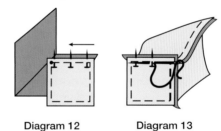

Diagram 12   Diagram 13

Bring the adjacent edge of the square up, and align it with the other edge of the angled unit. Insert a pin in each corner to align matching points; then pin the remainder of the seam (**Diagram 13**). Continuing the thread from the previous seam, hand-sew the seam from the corner to the open end of the angle, removing pins as you sew. Press the seam allowances of the set-in piece away from it.

MITER BORDERS

A border surrounds the piecework of many quilts. Mitered corners add to a border's frame effect.

To add a border with mitered corners, first pin a border strip to a quilt top edge, matching the center of the strip and the center of the quilt top edge. Allow excess border fabric to extend beyond the edges.

Sew together, beginning and ending the seam $1/4$" from the quilt top corners (**Diagram 14**). Repeat with the remaining border strips. Press the seam allowances toward the border strips.

Overlap the border strips at each corner (**Diagram 15**). Align the edge of a 90° right triangle with the raw edge of a top border strip so the long edge of the triangle intersects the seam in the corner. With a pencil, draw along the edge of the triangle from the border seam out to the raw edge. Place the bottom border strip on top, and repeat the marking process.

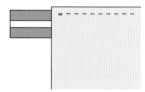

Diagram 14

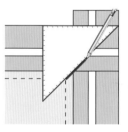

Diagram 15

With the right sides of adjacent border strips together, match the marked seam lines and pin (**Diagram 16**).

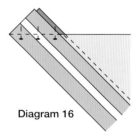

Diagram 16

Beginning with a backstitch at the inside corner, stitch exactly on the marked lines to the outside edges of the border strips. Check the right side of the corner to see that it lies flat. Then trim the excess fabric, leaving a $1/4$" seam allowance. Press the seam open. Mark and sew the remaining corners in the same manner.

Quilter's Schoolhouse

COMPLETE QUILT
Layering
Cut and piece backing fabric to measure at least 3" bigger on all sides than the quilt top. Press seams open. With wrong sides together, layer quilt top and backing fabric with the batting in between; baste. Quilt as desired.

Binding
Binding for most quilts is cut on the straight grain of the fabric. If your quilt has curved edges, cut the strips on the bias (see *page 156*). Cutting instructions for projects in this book specify the number of binding strips or a total length needed to finish the quilt. The instructions also specify enough width for a French-fold, or double-layer, binding because it's easier to apply and adds durability.

Join strips with diagonal seams to make one continuous binding strip (**Diagram 17**). Trim excess fabric, leaving $1/4$" seam allowances. Press seams open. Fold one end of the binding strip under 1" (**Diagram 18**); press. With wrong side inside, fold strip in half lengthwise and press (**Diagram 19**).

Beginning in the center of one edge, place binding strip against right side of quilt top, aligning binding strip's raw edges with quilt top's raw edge (**Diagram 20**). Beginning $1^1/2$" from the folded edge, sew through all layers, stopping $1/4$" from the corner. Backstitch; then clip threads. Remove quilt from under presser foot.

Fold binding strip upward (**Diagram 21**), creating a diagonal fold, and finger-press.

Holding diagonal fold in place with your finger, bring binding strip down in line with next edge of quilt top, making a horizontal fold that aligns with the quilt edge (**Diagram 22**).

Start sewing again at top of horizontal fold, stitching through all layers. Sew around quilt, turning each corner in the same manner.

When you return to starting point, encase binding strip's raw edge inside the folded end (**Diagram 23**). Finish sewing to starting point (**Diagram 24**). Trim batting and backing fabric even with quilt top edges.

Turn the binding over the edge to the back. Hand-stitch binding to backing fabric, making sure to cover all machine stitching.

To make mitered corners on the back, hand-stitch up to a corner; fold a miter in the binding. Take a stitch or two in the fold to secure it. Then stitch the binding in place up to the next corner. Finish each corner in the same manner.

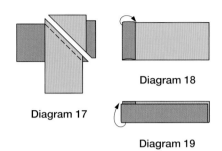

Diagram 17

Diagram 18

Diagram 19

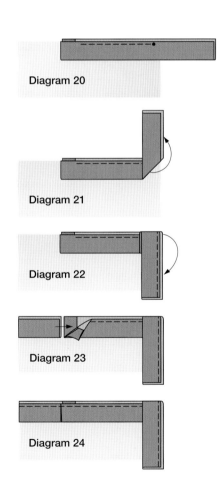

Diagram 20

Diagram 21

Diagram 22

Diagram 23

Diagram 24

PIPING
Piping, also known as covered cording, is made by sewing a fabric strip around a length of cording. The width of the strip varies according to the diameter of your cording. Refer to the specific project instructions for those measurements. Regardless, the method used to cover the cording is the same.

I. With the wrong side inside, fold under $1^1/2$" at one end of the strip. With the wrong side inside, fold the strip in half lengthwise to make the cording cover. Insert the cording next to the folded edge, placing a cording end 1" from the cording cover folded end. Using a cording foot or zipper foot, sew through all the fabric layers right next to the cording (**Diagram 25**).

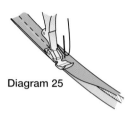

Diagram 25

2. When attaching the cording to your project, begin stitching $1^1/2$" from the covered cording's folded end. As you stitch each corner, clip the seam allowance to within a few threads of the stitching line; gently ease the covered cording into place (**Diagram 26**).

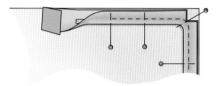

Diagram 26

3. After going around the entire edge of the project, cut the end of the cording so that it will fit snugly into the folded opening at the beginning (**Diagram 27**). The ends of the cording should abut inside the covering. Stitch the ends in place to secure (**Diagram 28**).

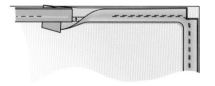

Diagram 27

Diagram 28

CREDITS

Quilt Designers

Autumn Ambience
Alma Allen & Barb Adams
of Blackbird Designs
blackbird-designs.blogspot.com

Autumn Bliss
Lisa Bongean
of Primitive Gatherings
primitivegatherings.us

Square Deal
Barbara Groves & Mary Jacobson
of Me and My Sister Designs
meandmysisterdesigns.com

Making Waves
Julie Hendricksen
of JJ Stitches
jjstitches.com

Rolling Stones, Vintage Voyage
Ann Hermes
of Ann Hermes Miniature Quilts
annhermesquilts.com

Links to Home
Miriam Kujac
Quilt collector

Bohemian Charm
Sarah Maxwell & Dolores Smith
of Homestead Hearth
homesteadhearth.com

Crossroads
Marti Michell
of From Marti Michell
frommarti.com

Scrappy Stars
Carrie Nelson
of Miss Rosie's Quilt Co.
missrosiesquiltco.com

Buggy Wheels
Janet Nesbitt & Pam Soliday
of The Buggy Barn
buggybarnquilts.com

Star Vine
Renée Plains
of Liberty Star
liberty-star.com

Meadow Blooms
Cynthia Tomaszewski
of Simple Pleasures
simpleas.com

Zen
Amy Walsh
of Blue Underground Studios
blueundergroundstudios.com

Laura Boehnke, *Quilt Tester*
With a keen color sense and an astute use of fabrics,
Laura tests each project in *American Patchwork & Quilting®*
magazine by making at least four blocks.

Credits

Project Makers & Quilters
Kelly Edwards: pages 14, 25, 48, 51, 85, 87, 114, 142, 144
Shelly Hall: pages 17, 36, 39, 112, 137
Lisa Ippolito: pages 14, 25, 48, 51, 134
Trina Kirkvold: page 105
Mary Korrect: pages 28, 61
Mary Pepper: pages 92, 105, 123
Patsy Preiss: pages 152, 154
Jan Ragaller: pages 66, 68, 114, 127
Nancy Sharr: page 57
Janelle Swenson: pages 57, 77, 79, 104
Cindy Tolliver: pages 17, 36, 66, 68, 112, 127
Jann Williams: pages 39, 94

Materials Suppliers
A.E. Nathan Company
Andover Fabrics
Benartex
Blank Quilting
Hoffman California Fabrics
Marcus Fabrics
Moda Fabrics
Northcott Silk
RJR Fabrics
Robert Kaufman Fabrics
Timeless Treasures Fabrics
Westminster Fabrics
Wilmington Prints

Photographers
Adam Albright: pages 14, 36, 48, 51, 66, 77, 78, 79, 85, 104, 105, 114, 123, 127, 134, 142, 144, 152
Craig Anderson: pages 13, 44, 47, 75, 119, 133
Marty Baldwin: pages 10, 32, 35, 50, 56, 58, 64, 65, 102, 113, 125, 135, 136, 155
Marcia Cameron pages 84, 138, 141
Kathryn Gamble: page 112
Andy Lyons: page 98
Blaine Moats: pages 23, 103, 110, 149
Cameron Sadeghpour: pages 17, 39, 52, 68, 72, 92, 94, 122, 131, 137

Greg Scheidemann: pages 25, 28, 30, 43, 57, 61, 63, 87, 88, 146, 154
Dean Schoeppner: page 24
Perry Struse: pages 8, 21, 82, 97, 109, 111, 116
Jay Wilde: pages 16, 19, 27, 54, 60, 67, 69, 86, 90, 91, 107, 143, 145